11+

SPELLING and VOCABULARY

Foundation Level

Book Three

Stephen C. Curran

and

Warren Vokes

This book belongs to:

....

Accelerated Education Publications

Exercise 47a

1) The cows had walked along the road to the **farm** and left it very muddy.

2) It was _____________ a long way to the shops that she had to catch a bus.

3) She sat at the mirror in her _____________ to comb her hair.

4) The toys were left outside but it did not rain and they came to no _____________ .

5) It was over thirty degrees in the _____________ and far too hot to play tennis.

6) He could feel the _____________ from the fire from across the room.

7) A very _____________ pile of magazines had been stacked on the coffee table.

8) With the lawn mown and trimmed the _____________ looked very tidy.

9) She broke the eggs into a bowl and then _____________ them with a whisk.

10) "_____________ you," she said as he sneezed for the second time.

Score / 10

Exercise 47b

11) I asked the price and it was much _____________ than I had expected.

12) "Close the _____________ , there's a draught in here."

13) "_____________ the green button and the gate will open."

14) The _____________ was selling newly laid eggs and she bought two dozen.

15) The salesman gave his business _____________ to the receptionist.

16) Chickens roamed freely around the _____________ at the back of the farmhouse.

17) Harvest was over and the _____________ was full with bales of hay.

18) She used the garden _____________ to sweep the fallen leaves from the patio.

19) Vegetarians don't eat _____________ .

20) He couldn't wait to use his bucket and _____________ on the beach. **Score** / 10

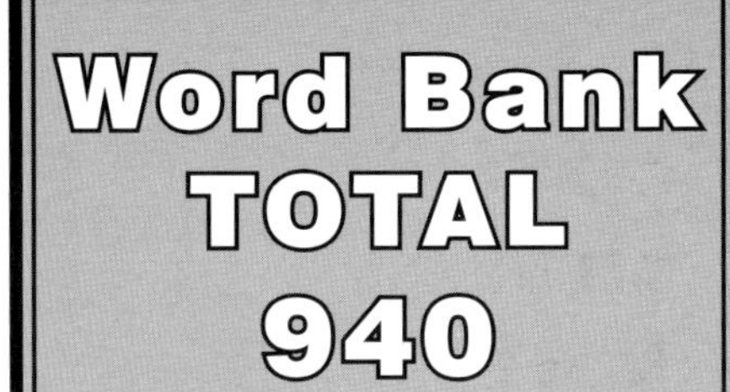

Word Bank TOTAL 940

Across

3. Enclosed paved piece of land.
5. Brush for sweeping.
6. Agricultural land and buildings.
7. Large farm outbuilding used for storage.
10. Cultivated area around a house.
11. Damage or injury.
12. Digging tool with handle and wide blade.
14. So much.
15. Smaller amount.
16. Glass covered opening in a building.
17. To hit repeatedly.

Down

1. Stiff paper with pictures and greetings.
2. Owner or operator of a farm.
4. A room for sleeping.
7. To make holy.
8. To push against something.
9. Edible animal flesh.
11. Energy felt as warmth or hotness.
12. Area out of direct sunlight.
13. Orderly in appearance.

47

Put the mystery letter (✳) into the box marked **47** below. Add in the mystery letters from puzzles **48** to **54** then rearrange them to make **Kate's Mystery Word**.

The clue is **ANIMAL**.

Enter your mystery letters here:

47	48	49	50	51	52	53	54

Now rearrange them:

Mystery Word:

Mystery Letter

Score /20

Across

48

1. A strip of material around the waist.
4. Perceived sounds.
5. Transparent.
6. Feeling of anxiety caused by danger.
7. Compass point opposite west.
9. Overtake.
11. A large animal.
13. The coloured part of a plant.
14. Flat green part of a plant or tree.
15. Pale reddish colour.

Down

1. Collection of things grouped or joined together.
2. Transparent solid substance used to make bottles, windows and lenses.
3. A group taught together.

Down (Continued)

6. A meal for many people to celebrate an occasion.
8. Densely populated area with many buildings.
9. A bucket.
10. Large piece of fabric used on a boat to catch the wind.
11. Colour between red and yellow.
12. To use the mind to form thoughts.
13. Level and horizontal without any slope.

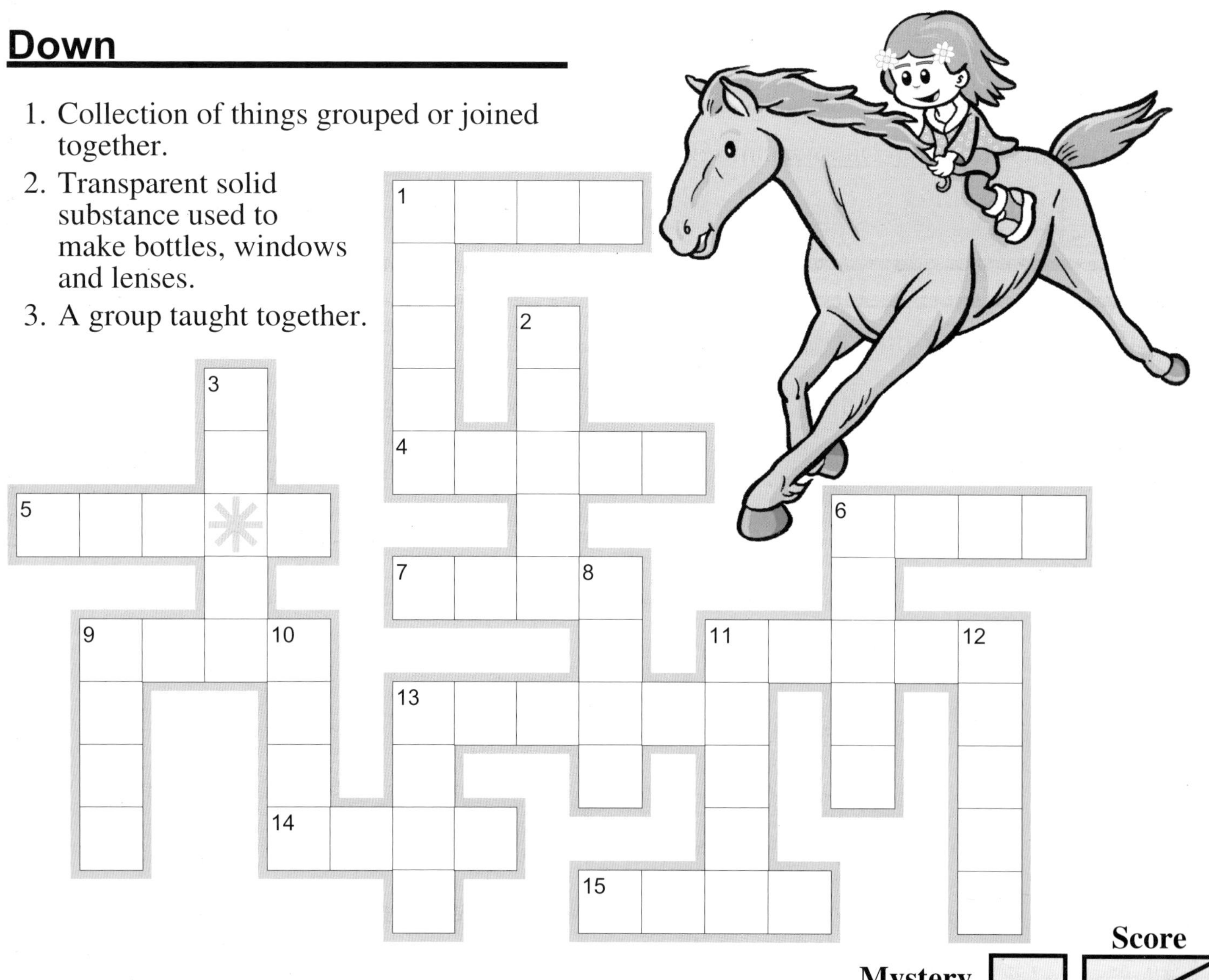

Mystery Letter

Score / 20

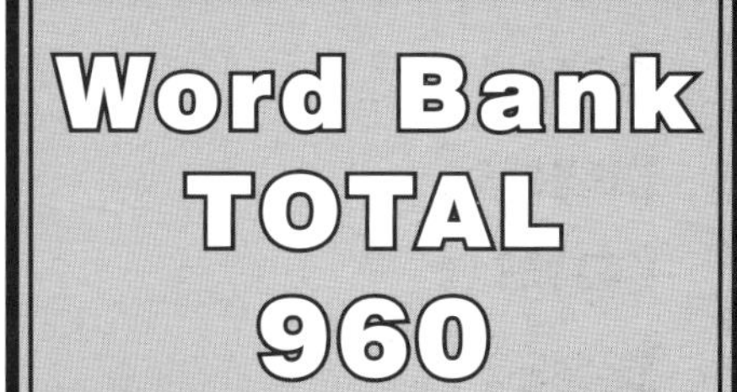

pink	think
flat	east
feast	beast
sail	pail

Exercise 48a

1) He was really frightened and the _____________ could be seen on his face.

2) The newspapers referred to the animal as the '_____________ *of Bodmin Moor'*.

3) It was a large _____________ of flowers that she had picked that morning.

4) The _____________ autumn leaves that had fallen from the trees littered the streets.

5) The albino rabbit's nose was very ___________ and his fur was pure white.

6) The window had been broken and pieces of _____________ were lying on the ground.

7) The driver _____________ the guard's whistle, saw the green flag and released the brake.

8) "Could you please _____________ me the cruet. I would like some pepper on my meal."

9) Through the ___________ water of the stream he saw the fish swimming past.

10) The ___________ had been eaten by the caterpillars.

Score ⬛ /10

Exercise 48b

11) Their _____________ went on a school journey to the science museum.

12) The ship headed _____________ as the sun sank below the horizon behind its stern.

13) It was market day and the ___________ was full of people looking for a bargain.

14) "Make sure you always wear your seat ___________ when travelling in the car."

15) The earth was believed to be _____________ before it was circumnavigated.

16) All the plants were beginning to _____________ in the warm sunshine.

17) The wind picked up and the yacht's ___________ billowed out as it gathered speed.

18) "I didn't _____________ anybody had heard me but help arrived soon after I called out.

19) A huge _____________ was held in the great hall to celebrate their success.

20) He used the metal___________ to fetch water for the animals.

Score ⬛ /10

Exercise 49a

1) The horse had gone ______________ and he had to dismount and walk instead.

2) After using this book he found that he was _________________ all the words correctly.

3) The pneumatic ____________ that they were using to dig up the road was very loud.

4) It was only a ______________ and when he awoke there was no one else in the room.

5) Apple _________ was his favourite dessert but for a change he ordered the gâteau.

6) The rabbit was very ______________ and liked children holding and stroking it.

7) She could not ___________ to be noticed wearing such a huge wide-brimmed hat.

8) "The ______________ you could do is offer to help clear up your mess!"

9) "I didn't mean to ______________ my drink. It was an accident!"

10) "It was your fault and you must take the ______________ ."

Score [/10]

Exercise 49b

11) "Make sure you water the plants or they will _________ in this heat."

12) He had been caught and hung his head in ______________ as they led him away.

13) He hung his jacket on an old rusty __________ which stuck out from the door.

14) "Would you like some _______________ with your strawberries?" the waiter asked.

15) After they had finished the ______________ he asked the waiter for the bill.

16) The wicked witch cast her evil ______________ on the beautiful princess.

17) It was a ______ when he said he had not see them. He'd spoken to them before they left.

18) Our hotel swimming ______________ was very crowded so we went to the beach instead.

19) "Here, ______________ this pastille it will help to soothe your sore throat."

20) The pancake ______________ contained flour, eggs and milk.

Score [/10]

meal	**spelling**
shame	**suck**
die	**pie**
lie	**pool**

Word Bank TOTAL 980

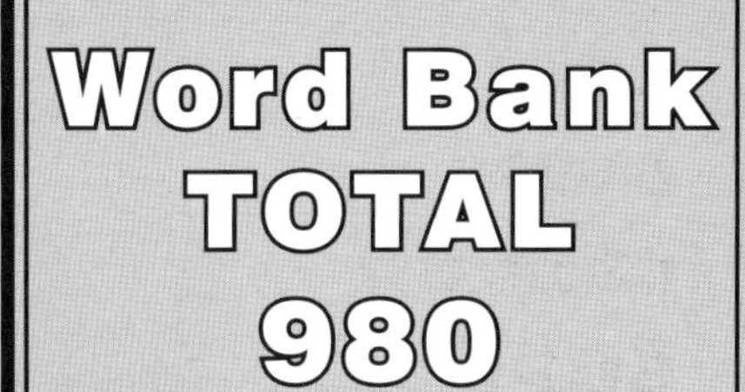

Across

49

3. The fatty part of milk.
4. To name or write in correct order the letters of a word.
5. To be unsuccessful.
7. To deliberately say something untrue.
9. Accidentally allow something to flow from a container.
10. To stop living.
12. Images that appear to the mind while asleep.
14. Forming words with letters.
15. A small body of still water.

Down

1. No longer wild.
2. A substantial amount of food eaten at one time.
4. A state of disgrace or dishonour.
6. The smallest amount possible.
7. Walking unevenly because of a leg injury.
8. To consider someboby responsible for something wrong that has happened.
11. Strong pointed metal pin hammered into wood or masonry.
12. Rotating piece of metal that bores holes.
13. To combine ingredients.
14. To draw liquid out with the mouth.
15. Baked dish consisting of a filling enclosed in or covered with pastry.

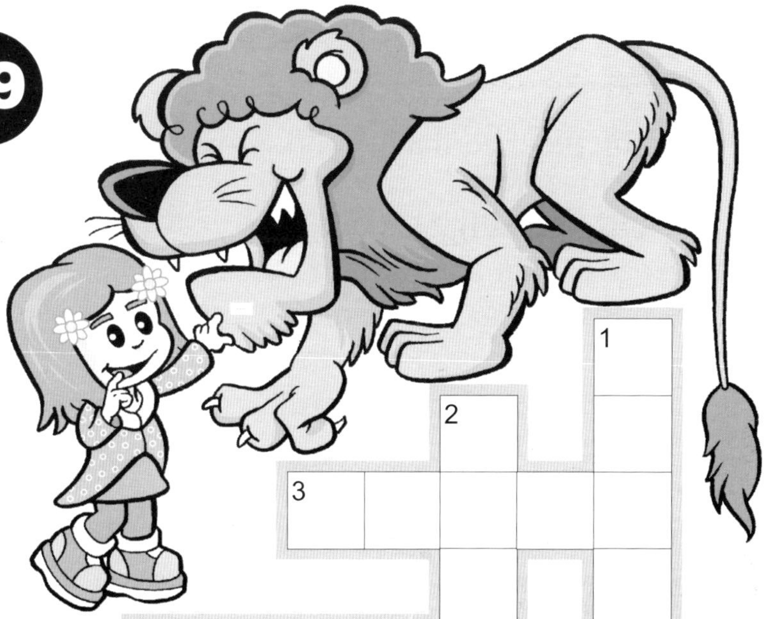

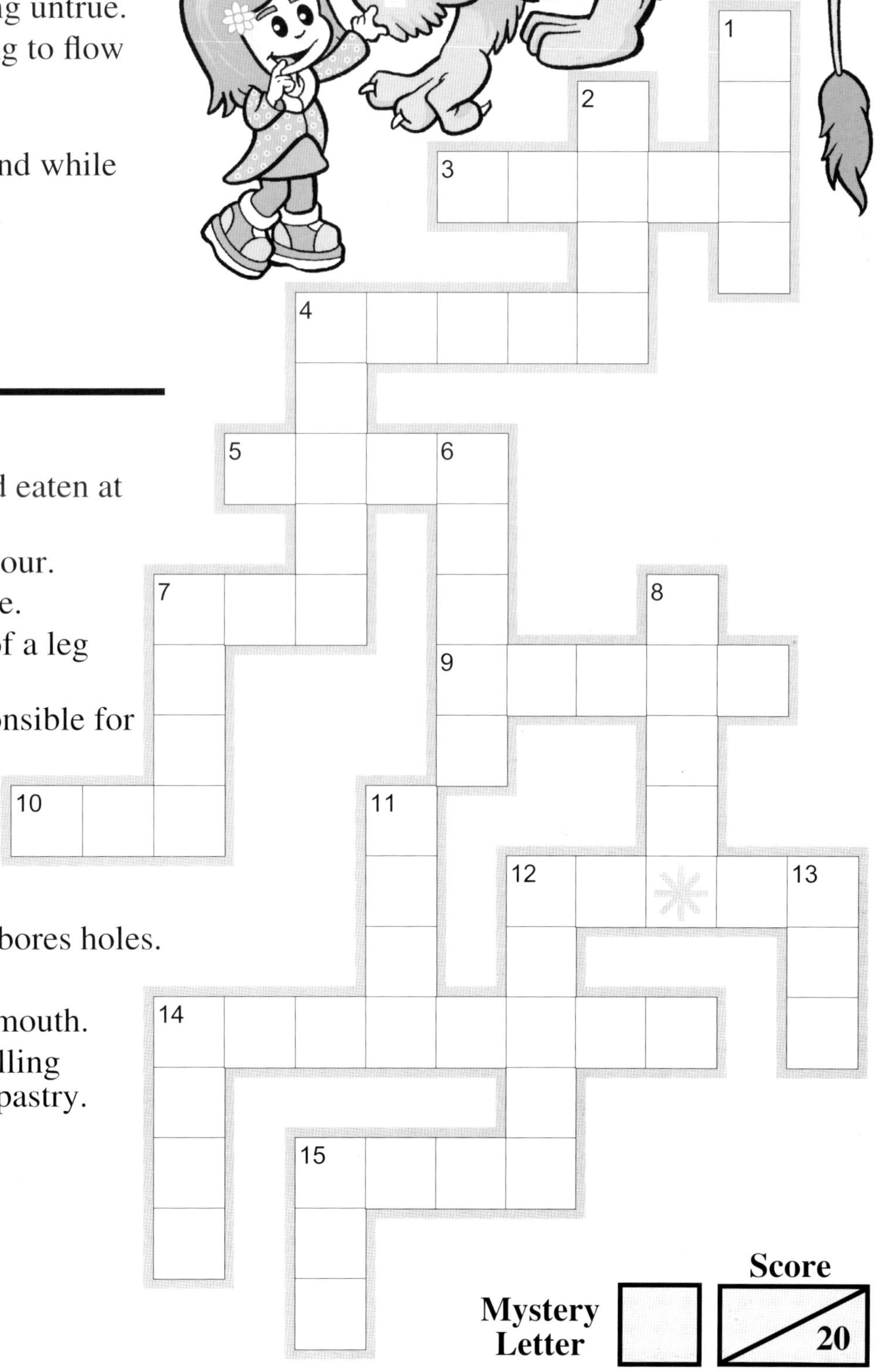

Mystery Letter

Score /20

Across

50

1. A substance, normally solid, providing nourishment.
4. Coldish. Usually pleasantly so.
7. To cause pain.
8. To move to face a different direction.
10. A polite form of address to a man.
11. A tree bearing acorns as fruit.
12. An article of clothing for the upper body.
14. Ceased to exist.
17. Something heavy or bulky carried or transported.
18. The end of being alive.

Down

1. Compact and solid when pressed.
2. An unclean substance.
3. To be or to set on fire.
4. To bend, twist or wind something into a curved or spiral shape.
5. False statements made deliberately.
6. A building for public worship.
9. Prepared for something that is going to happen.
13. One of three equal parts.
15. No longer alive.
16. A horned mammal related to sheep.

Mystery Letter

Score

20

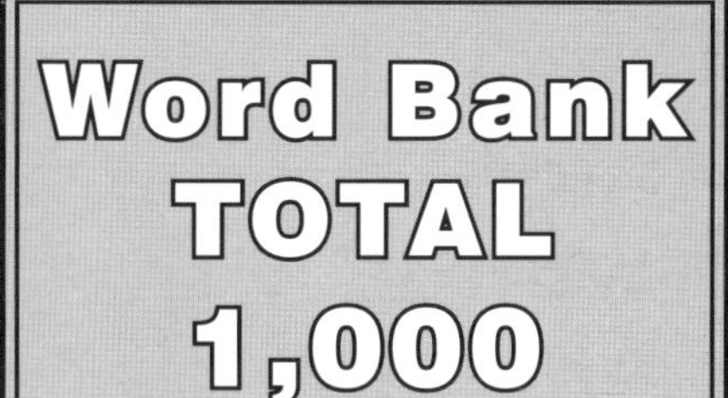

Exercise 50a

1) Following the ______________ of the king, his eldest son acceded to the throne.

2) "Please _________ , may I leave the classroom?" he asked the teacher.

3) The squirrel was collecting acorns from the ___________ tree to store for the winter.

4) The forest fire continued to ___________ and they could only hope it would soon rain.

5) They were so well matched they crossed the line together in a ___________ heat.

6) He was being collected at seven o'clock but he was ______________ long before.

7) It is customary for the bride to arrive at the _________________ late for her wedding.

8) The auctioneer asked for the ____________ and last time and banged his gavel. "Sold!"

9) The fan helped to keep them ______________ in the hot weather.

10) "The collar on this new ______________ is making my neck sore."

Score / 10

Exercise 50b

11) "Could you help me ___________ these suitcases onto the roof rack?"

12) An old nanny ______________ was chained to a stake at the edge of the field.

13) When he got to his feet he brushed the ___________ from the knees of his trousers.

14) He took the free kick and managed to ___________ the ball around the goalkeeper.

15) "The place you want __________ at the foot of those hills you can see over there."

16) " ______________ again Whittington, Lord Mayor of London."

17) The hotel bed was very __________ and he preferred a softer mattress.

18) Her pet hamster had ___________ and her parents took her to buy another one.

19) The rugby player wrenched his knee and it ___________ when he stood up.

20) The favourite ____________ of the giant panda is bamboo shoots.

Score / 10

Exercise 51a

1) The ____________ was high in the tree and its caw could be heard across the landscape.

2) The north __________ shines brighter than the rest and is easy to identify.

3) The windows in the rooms __________________ overlooked the garden next door.

4) It was a _________ bridge and the lorry had struck the brickwork and become stuck.

5) They went ______________ , closed the door and waited for it to stop raining.

6) It was a cold, wet ____________ and they longed for the warmth of the morning sun.

7) There were a ___________ of brass candlesticks for sale in the antique shop.

8) "Don't _______________ to send me a postcard from Cyprus when you are away."

9) They made very ______________ progress along the steep and muddy path.

10) The cannon fired to signal the ______________ of the yacht race.   **Score** ☐ 10

Exercise 51b

11) I can't decide whether to see the matinée or go to _______________ 's performance.

12) The weather _________________ was atrocious and they decided to stay indoors.

13) The __________ tread creaked when he placed his foot on it.

14) "Write down this ______________ , look it up in the dictionary and tell me its meaning."

15) He heard a sound in the night and went ___________________ to investigate.

16) The car turned ______________ at the crossroads and headed away from the town centre.

17) The _________ was leaking from the tyre and it was slowly deflating.

18) Sir Francis Chichester was the first lone yachtsman to sail around the ______________ .

19) "All burglaries must be reported to the police _____________ 24 hours."

20) "His is a very ______________ pupil and should do well here."   **Score** ☐ 10

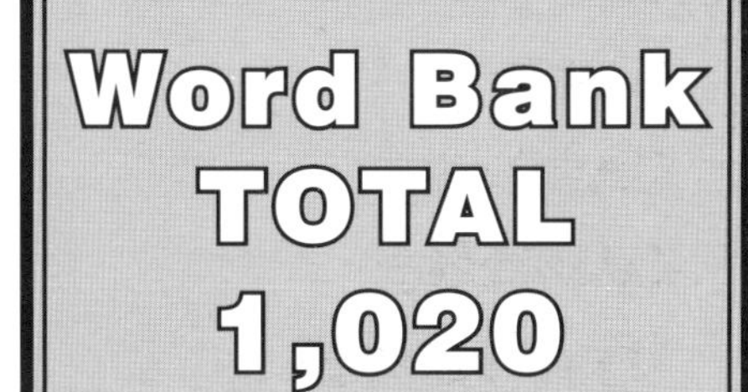

inside
within
slow
star
outside
low
crow
start

Word Bank TOTAL 1,020

51

Across

1. Earth and everything on it.
4. Not moving quickly.
6. The internal part of something.
9. Large bird with shiny black feathers and a raucous cry.
11. Giving off strong light.
12. A flight of steps leading from one level to another.
15. Two matching objects that are designed to be used together.
16. The night or evening of the present day.
17. To, towards, or on an upper level.
20. Unit of langauge either spoken or written.

Down

2. To, towards, or on a lower level.
3. The mixture of gases that forms the Earth's atmosphere.
5. Close to the ground.
7. The entire period between sunset and sunrise.
8. To fail to remember something.
10. The outer surface or appearance of something.
13. The east when facing north.
14. Somebody or something is inside.
18. Point of light in the night sky.
19. To begin.

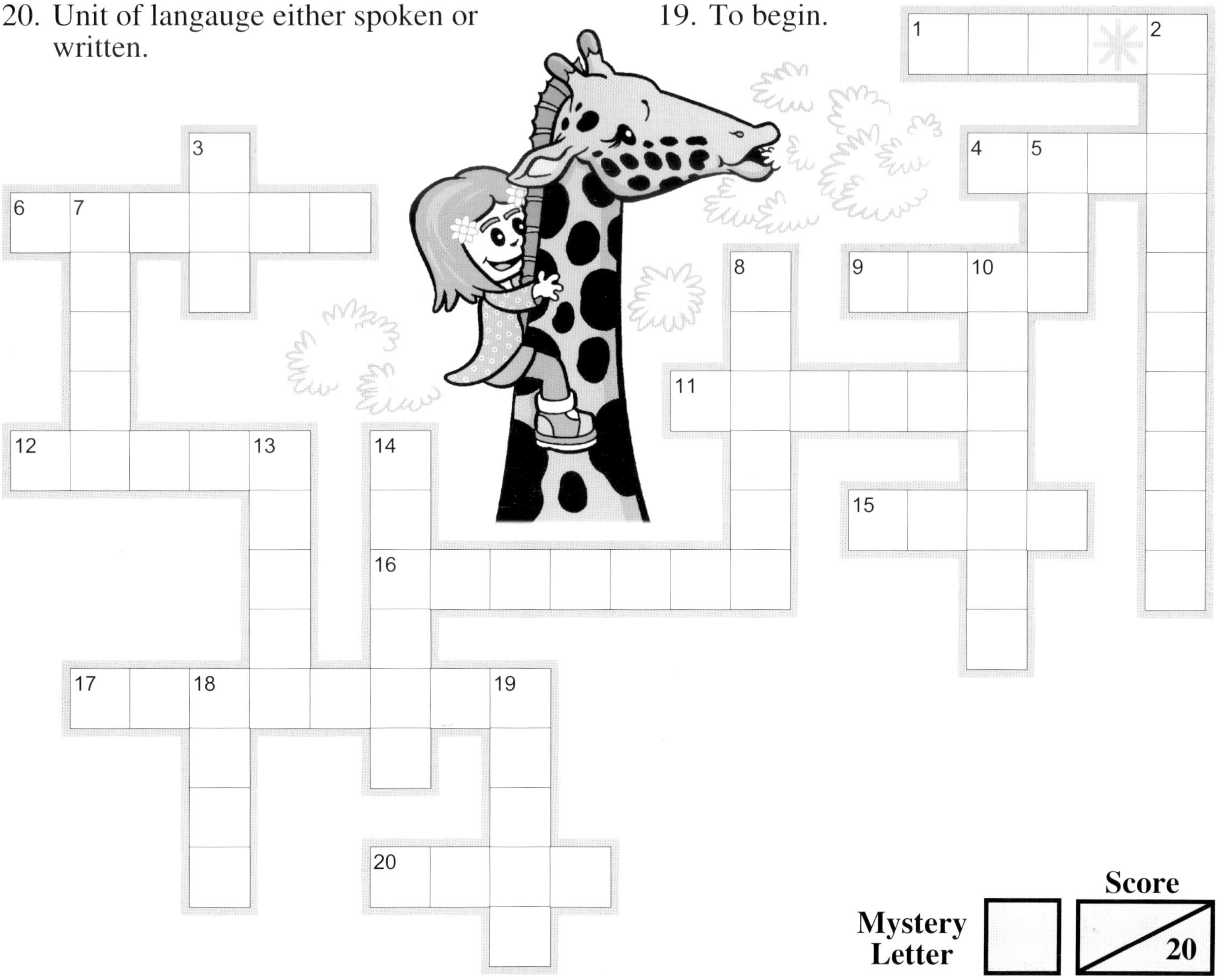

Mystery Letter

Score /20

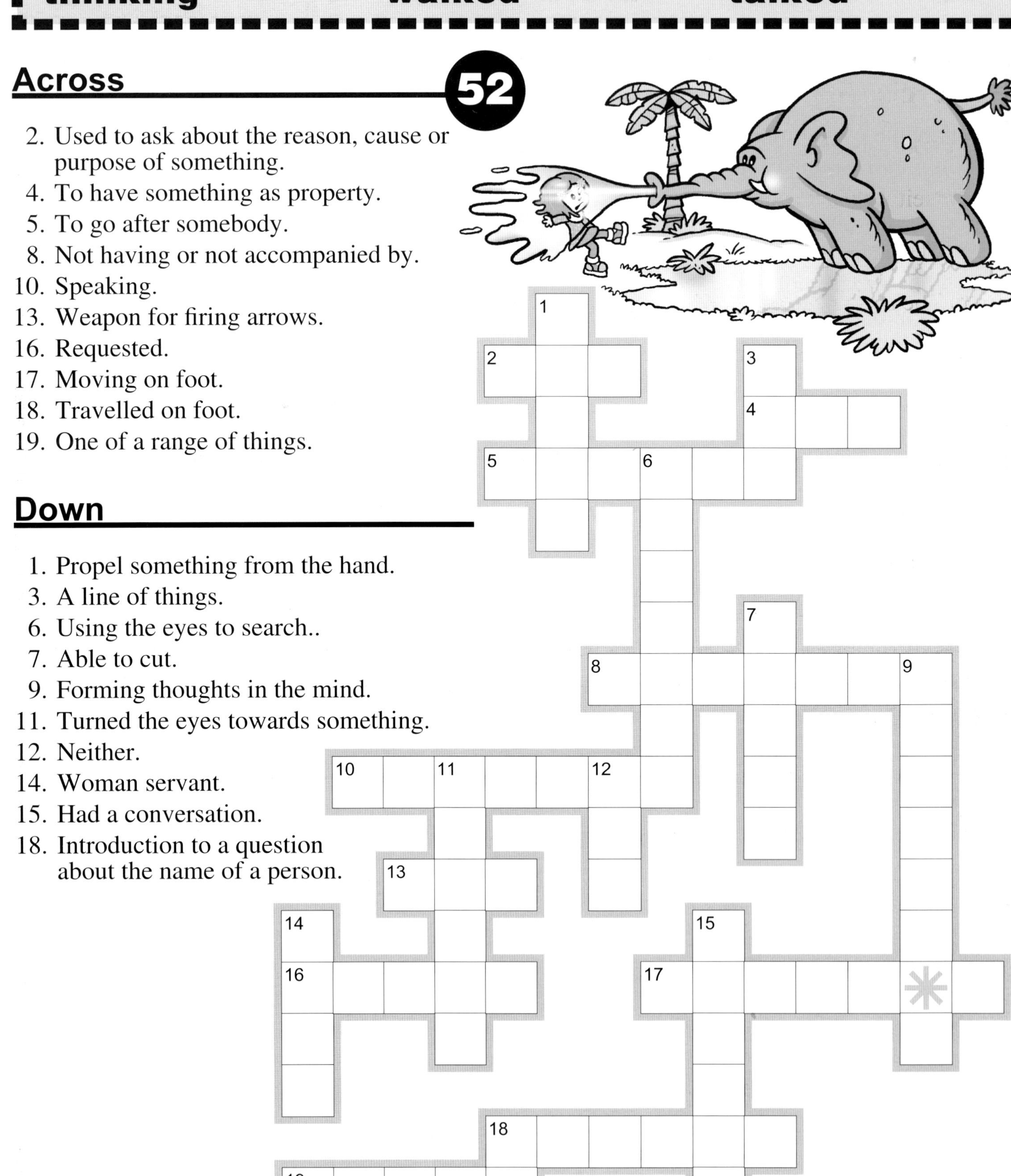

Across

52

2. Used to ask about the reason, cause or purpose of something.
4. To have something as property.
5. To go after somebody.
8. Not having or not accompanied by.
10. Speaking.
13. Weapon for firing arrows.
16. Requested.
17. Moving on foot.
18. Travelled on foot.
19. One of a range of things.

Down

1. Propel something from the hand.
3. A line of things.
6. Using the eyes to search..
7. Able to cut.
9. Forming thoughts in the mind.
11. Turned the eyes towards something.
12. Neither.
14. Woman servant.
15. Had a conversation.
18. Introduction to a question about the name of a person.

Score

Mystery Letter

20

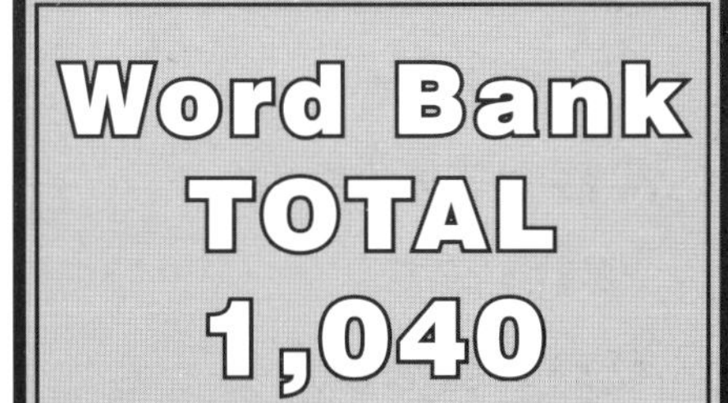

Exercise 52a

1) "Do you know ____________ left that there for us to trip over?" asked the headmaster.

2) Neither the workman __________ the lorry driver could find the wheelbarrow.

3) The cars were parked in a ___________ that was at least 10 metres long.

4) The audience continued to applaud and the cast took another ____________ .

5) They had a lot of news for each other and they _____________ for ages.

6) They _______________ slowly along the river bank studying the water fowl.

7) He rang for the ____________ and asked her to bring them tea and cakes.

8) "Don't _______________ sand at each other. It will get in your eyes!"

9) I was not clear ___________ the signal had failed to operate.

10) My cat was sitting on the window sill _______________ at the birds. **Score** /10

Exercise 52b

11) I spent many hours _______________ to the old man about his life on the canals.

12) He had entered _________________ permission and was arrested for trespassing.

13) He had been _________________ for many hours before he came to the village.

14) "Try to complete the exercises on your _____________ but ask me if you need help."

15) It __________________ certain that they would win but then they conceded a goal.

16) She had _____________ for black coffee but it came with milk.

17) The blade was very _____________ and it cut through the rope with ease.

18) She was not sure _____________ blouse to buy as she liked them both.

19) "I was _______________ I might call in and see you as I'm passing."

20) We tried to _______________ the path but it became very overgrown. **Score** /10

13

Exercise 53a

1) After the heavy rainfall the water butt was ____________ to overflowing.

2) The ____________ chops in the butcher's window looked very good value.

3) A large black ____________ passed overhead and obscured the sun.

4) Despite being very ill the sick animal was still ____________ the following day.

5) It was a very cold ____________ wind that blew down from the artic circle.

6) There was a small ____________ in the hedge which he could just squeeze through.

7) He could see the cows were gathered all ____________ the edge of the field.

8) "Mind where you walk and don't ____________ over that tree stump in the ground."

9) She rang the ____________ 's surgery to make an appointment.

10) Please could you ____________ louder, I'm a little deaf."

Score ☐ 10

Exercise 53b

11) The standard unit of currency in ____________ Africa is the rand.

12) They had turned the wrong way at the ____________ in the road.

13) Her appointment was three o'clock but an ____________ later she had still not been seen.

14) "That music is far too ____________ , please could you turn it down."

15) It was a secret and they were ____________ to each other very quietly.

16) She was sitting in her favourite chair ____________ another chapter from the novel.

17) He ____________ aware of a sound behind him, turned and saw them approaching.

18) She had ____________ her skirt several times but the stain refused to come out.

19) The jockey used his ____________ to drive the horse on towards the finish.

20) The door ____________ onto a small patio that faced due south.

Score ☐ 10

Across

53

2. The flesh of a pig eaten as food.
4. A thin strip of leather attached to a handle.
6. In a particular direction.
8. Involving speech.
10. Living and not dead.
11. 60 minutes.
13. One of the cardinal points on a compass.
15. Somebody qualified to give medical treatment.
16. Changed or developed.
17. A mass of water particles in the sky.
19. Identifying written words.

Down

1. Utter words.
3. A gap.
5. A journey.
7. Cleaned with water.
8. Compass point opposite north.

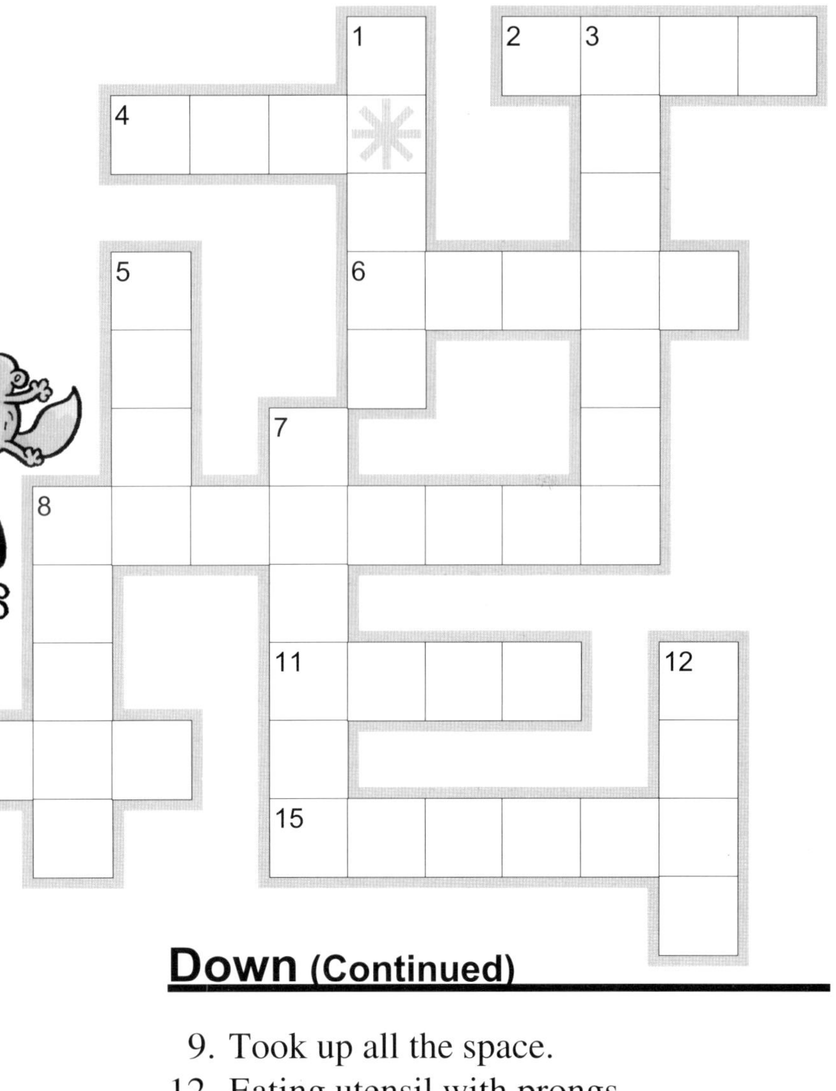

Down (Continued)

9. Took up all the space.
12. Eating utensil with prongs.
14. Not closed or locked.
18. High in volume or sound.

Mystery Letter

Score
20

Across

54

2. Passing something to somebody.
3. A social gathering for fun.
7. Game played by kicking or heading a round ball.
10. Walk in military fashion.
12. Short works of fiction.
15. A colour between yellow and blue.
16. Recently made.
17. Large container to sit in and wash your body.
18. Man in position of authority.
19. A series of rhythmical steps and body movements.

Down

1. Extremely small.
4. White boney object in the mouth.
5. Women.

Down (Continued)

6. Possessing or owning.
8. Alive, not dead.
9. Very young children who cannot yet walk or talk.
11. Outdoor play area with swings, slides and seesaws.
13. Used for biting and chewing food.
14. Examined, looked at or watched using the eyes.
17. A woven container with a handle.

! Don't forget to go back to page **3** and complete **Kate's Mystery Word.**

Mystery Letter

Score
20

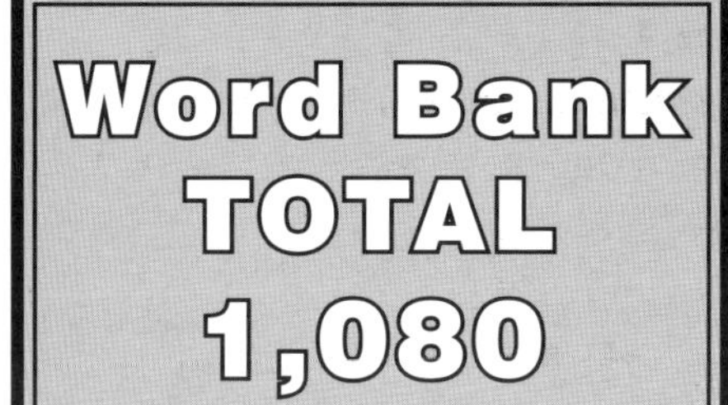

Exercise 54a

1) The old sailor told incredible ______________ about his exploits at sea.

2) He had lost most of his ____________ and had great difficulty chewing.

3) Only one broken, yellowing ___________ remained at the front of his mouth.

4) The maternity ward was full of new ____________ and the sound of their crying.

5) The small boy would ___________ up and down and pretend to be a soldier.

6) It was a fine day and perfect weather for playing cricket on the village ___________ .

7) It was too wet to go out into the _________________ so we had to stay in school.

8) England won the international _____________ match against France by two goals.

9) She had a warm, relaxing _____________ and went to bed early.

10) He was ______________ his hair cut at the barber's.

Score ____ / 10

Exercise 54b

11) "Your worship the Mayor, _____________ and gentlemen. Good evening to you all."

12) I asked him but he was ___________ nothing away and ignored my question.

13) They hadn't ___________ each other for many years but he still recognized her.

14) The highlight of Jennifer's birthday was the ___________ in the evening.

15) It was a very grand house and had a huge ________________ bedroom.

16) We sat on the sofa in the __________ room and opened the photograph album.

17) It was just like _________ and sparkled in the bright lights of the shop window.

18) He looked down at her. Compared with his own, the little baby's hand was ______ .

19) The 'Charleston' was a ___________ that was all the rage in the 1920's.

20) She was frail and used a shopping _____________ with wheels.

Score ____ / 10

17

At the Office

Can you find all these words in the picture below? Write in the correct word against each number as you find them.

chart	swivel chair	desk lamp	bin	extinguisher
fan	lift	manager	pot plant	blind
briefcase	first aid kit	skyscraper	report	receptionist

1.______________________   2.______________________   3.______________________

4.______________________   5.______________________   6.______________________

7.______________________   8.______________________   9.______________________

10._____________________   11._____________________   12._____________________

13._____________________   14._____________________   15._____________________

In the Street

Can you find all these words in the picture below? Write in the correct word against each number as you find them.

wall	hedge	bungalow	aerial	bicycle
removal lorry	roof	flower bed	garage	carport
chimney	'Sold' board	lamp post	motor scooter	shed

1.____________________ 2.____________________ 3.____________________

4.____________________ 5.____________________ 6.____________________

7.____________________ 8.____________________ 9.____________________

10.____________________ 11.____________________ 12.____________________

13.____________________ 14.____________________ 15.____________________

Exercise 55a

1) There was a thorn in the dog's ____________ and the vet had to remove it.

2) I prefer ____________ my bicycle to school than going by bus.

3) My mother found an old ____________ mould shaped like a rabbit in a charity shop.

4) His legs really ached but he ____________ on running determined to win.

5) Curry with ____________ is one of my favourite meals.

6) As we cannot go today, I have arranged to go out ____________ with my brother.

7) "A very ____________ Christmas to you all!" he cried.

8) The paint she had chosen for the garage door was a bright ____________ red.

9) I gave her a pound and she gave me nineteen ____________ change.

10) Joshua struggled to ____________ his heavy bag to school.

Score 10

Exercise 55b

11) "Look at the birds stripping the ____________ from the shrubs to eat."

12) Her shoe got caught in a drain and the high ____________ was ripped off.

13) "I expect I ____________ see you again at the club meeting next week."

14) Only one mouse was white, the other ____________ were brown.

15) He was very embarassed and did not ____________ that he deserved such praise.

16) The man was very friendly with a ____________ face and big red cheeks.

17) She only needed to be shown ____________ and she could do it for herself.

18) My dad told me that he asked mum to ____________ him when they were only eighteen.

19) A fruit bowl full of shiny red ____________ stood on the sideboard.

20) A ____________ is a small, juicy fruit.

Score 10

Word Bank TOTAL 1,100

Across   55

1. Intended to happen.
4. Friendly and cheerful.
7. Small round fruit with a single hard stone.
8. To take somebody in marriage.
11. Edible grains from the plant of the same name served hot or cold after cooking in water.
13. Being on a horse.
14. A four-legged animal's foot.
15. Touch something.
16. More than one cherry.
17. Small rodents with a brown or greyish-brown coat and a long hairless tail.

Down

2. Back part of the foot.
3. To hold and transport.
4. A wobbly fruit flavoured dessert.
5. Small juicy, fleshy fruit.
6. The next day.
7. Taken to another place.
9. Lively and cheerful.
10. Any small juicy fruits.
12. At a time in the past.
14. Term for the unit of money used in Britain since 1971.

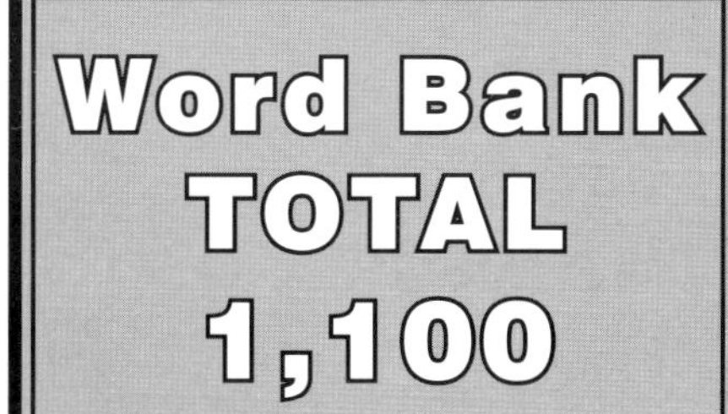

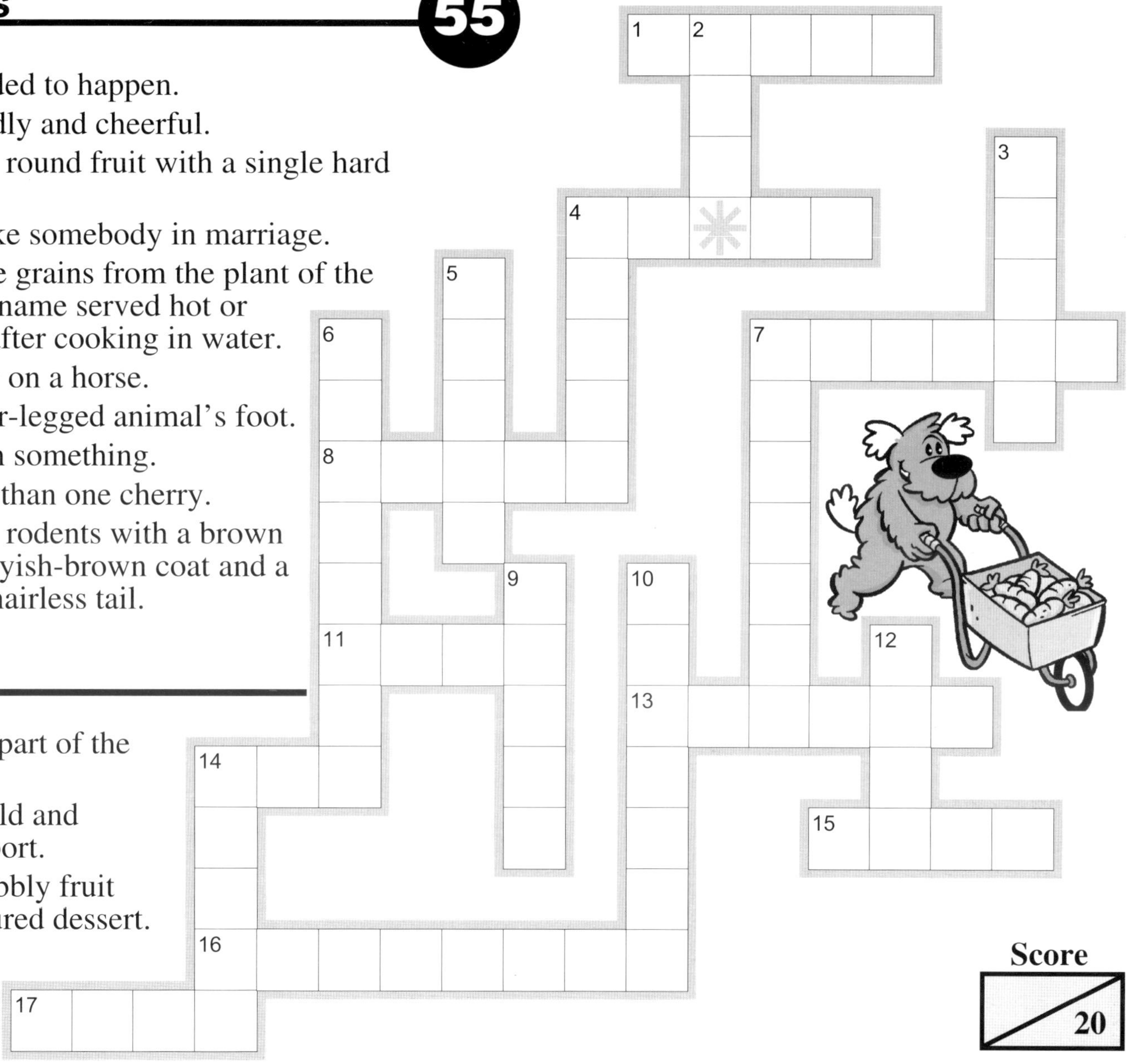

Score / 20

Put the mystery letter (✳) into box **55** below. Add in the mystery letters from puzzles **56** to **61** then rearrange them to make **Dicken's Mystery Word**. The clue is **VEGETABLE**.

Enter your mystery letters here:

55	56	57

58	59	60	61

Now rearrange them:

Mystery Word:

Across

56

4. A plant with edible pods and seeds.
5. To give pleasure or satisfaction to somebody.
8. Not difficult.
9. Shedding tears.
13. Conducts a legal case in court.
14. To go ahead and show the way.
15. To stretch out or extend as far as a particular point.
16. Attempted.
18. To make a picture.

Down

1. Unwilling to spend money on other people.
2. Quite hot.
3. Travels in an aircraft.
4. A strip of sand or pebbles at the point where the land meets the sea.

Down (Continued)

6. Without excess fat.
7. Brightly coloured.
9. Makes a distinctive sound.
10. Very large and impressive.
11. Called out loudly.
12. Spheres pierced for stringing on a necklace.
17. Uncooked.

Mystery Letter

Score 20

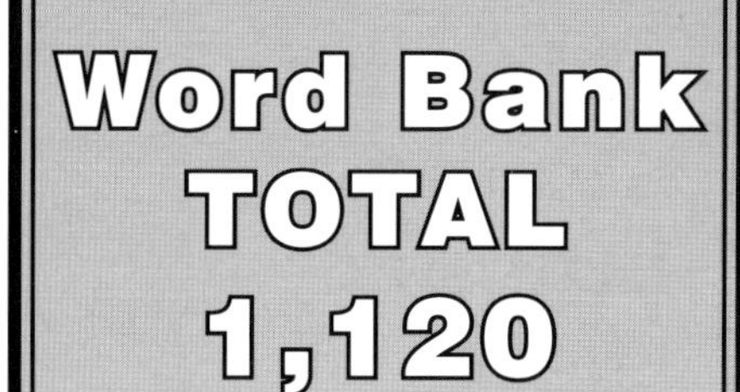

Exercise 56a

1) By standing on a chair he could just _____________ the top of the cupboard.

2) The meat was very undercooked and almost __________ so he sent it back.

3) The street looked very __________ with brightly coloured bunting and flags.

4) He has his own light aircraft and __________ to Le Tourquet every weekend.

5) She did all she could to _______________ him but he still found fault with her.

6) My sister is really _____________ , she won't share her sweets with me.

7) Simon found the test quite _____________ but Jason found it difficult.

8) Her necklace broke and the _______________ fell to the ground and went everywhere.

9) "Let's go to the _______________ , it's a lovely day for swimming."

10) Her baby was hungry and _______________ for attention.

Score [/10]

Exercise 56b

11) The distinctive _______________ of hyenas could be heard from far away.

12) The thermos flask had kept the coffee _____________ and it tasted very good.

13) "I've really ____________ hard to improve but I don't seem to get any better."

14) Around the final bend she took the _____________ and went on to win the race.

15) Isambard Kingdom Brunel completed many __________ engineering projects.

16) "I wish I could ____________ and paint like my art teacher."

17) We put a __________ onto a wet sheet of kitchen roll and after a few days it sprouted.

18) The bacon rashers were very _____________ with hardly any fat at all.

19) Whenever my friend tells a joke he __________ hard not to laugh.

20) The wounded animal was __________ out in pain.

Score [/10]

Exercise 57a

1) My dad and I used to go out just ________________ dawn to look for mushrooms.

2) He ________________ to his knees behind the bushes and raised his binoculars.

3) They arrived on Thursday, __________ days before the weekend.

4) "Fetch my ________________ for me and help me take my shoes off," said granddad.

5) She was ________________ really wet and wished she had remembered her umbrella.

6) Is there __________________ I can get for you from the supermarket when I go?"

7) They were all very large but by far the __________________ was Brian's.

8) There were not ________________ bracelets on display so she asked to see some more.

9) "You look very tired, it's ________________ you stay here and rest."

10) Down ________________ the ship's hold was full of machinery.

Score 10

Exercise 57b

11) She enjoyed __________________ with her friends turning the rope.

12) She pulled the blanket tighter around her but she still ___________ cold.

13) It was September and the conkers were ________________ from the horse chestnut trees.

14) My mum always made sure that there was ____________ fruit in the bowl for us to eat.

15) He had left the water ________________ and the bath was almost overflowing.

16) "Do you have ____________ more cornflakes? This box is empty."

17) The blazer did not ____________ to anyone there so he handed it in as lost property.

18) The rain had ________________ earlier but the grass was still much too wet to cut.

19) It was obvious from the look on __________ faces that they were guilty.

20) I gave the ________________ of the two bananas to Rachel.

Score 10

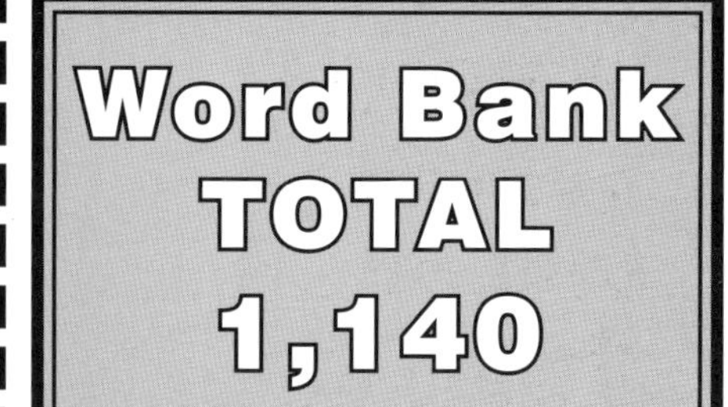

before
belong
many
fresh
below
any
anything
felt

Word Bank TOTAL 1,140

57

Across

2. A fabric made from wool or animal hair.
4. A considerable number.
6. Every person or thing stated.
8. Belonging to them.
9. Not old or stale.
13. Jumping over a circling rope.
15. Earlier than a particular date, time or event.
16. Bringing or obtaining.
17. Fallen from a higher place.
18. Rapid movement on foot.

Down

1. More pleasing or acceptable.
3. The number 2.
5. Any object, event, action, situation, or fact.
7. Situated or placed beneath something.
10. Came to a standstill.
11. Of greater size, number or amount.
12. Letting go of something.
13. A flat soft shoe usually worn indoors.
14. To be somebody's property.
15. Of greatest size, number or amount.

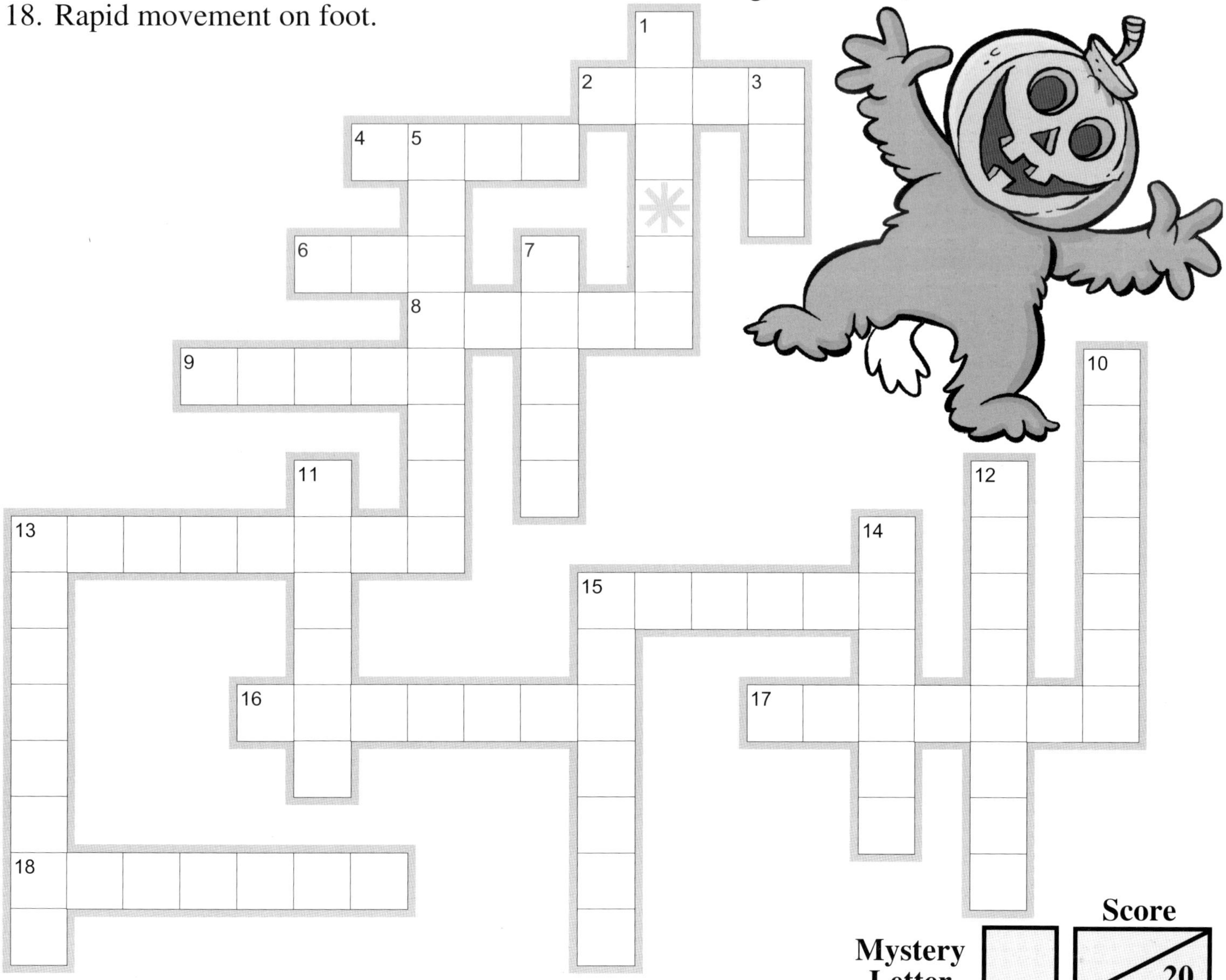

Mystery Letter

Score
20

Across

58

4. In a position next to.
5. Tied firmly together.
6. To cause a liquid to reach the temperature at which it turns to gas.
7. Held in your possession.
9. Water droplets on cool outdoor surfaces.
10. Believed firmly.
12. To bring or come together.
13. Indicates separation or distance between two points.
15. Made a picture using a pencil.
16. A zero quantity.

Down

1. At the back or rear.
2. Something that can be heard.
3. To change a substance from a solid to a liquid state by heating it.
5. Moved as a current of air.
8. Unit of currency used in the United Kingdom.
10. To be certain about something.
11. Indicate with an extended finger.
14. Not many.
17. Thick greasy liquid.
18. Became larger.

Mystery Letter

Score /20

Exercise 58a

1) "Over a low heat, ___________ the butter in the omlette pan then add the beaten eggs."

2) Sophie wanted to ___________ in the game but she didn't know the rules.

3) He was not very sociable and very much __________ himself to himself.

4) The poacher _______________ from experience where to find game to catch illegally.

5) "Something is _______________ to turn up," said Mr Macawber.

6) There were only a _________ left and they would not be enough to make a pie.

7) The gate hinges were squeaking but applying the _________ silenced them.

8) The _______________ of heavy footsteps echoed down the street and then I saw him!

9) "I know you have it hidden _______________ your back. Show me your hands."

10) Somewhere _________ to his left he heard a low whistle.

Score ___/10

Exercise 58b

11) The artillery continued relentlessly to _________________ the enemy's position.

12) "Allow the water to come to the ___________ before putting in the egg."

13) Without turning his head, he could see she had sat down _______________ him.

14) The instructor used a pencil to _____________ to the features on the map.

15) He ____________ his nose rather loudly and everyone turned towards him.

16) "Do you ___________ where they have gone this afternoon? Did they tell you?"

17) The early morning _________ had made his boots wet as he walked across the field.

18) She seized his arm, ___________ the boy towards her and whispered softly in his ear.

19) There is _________________ more refreshing than a good night's sleep.

20) The trees _____________ to over ten metres high.

Score ___/10

Exercise 59a

1) The dog was ill, had lost weight and looked very ____________ .

2) Always ___________ sun cream to protect you from the effects of ultra violet rays.

3) "See ___________ houses over there, I lived in the middle one."

4) There was a tail wind and their flight arrived _______________ .

5) The cart was pulled by two ____________ led by a young barefoot boy.

6) The water was so clear we ___________ see that the bottom was rocky.

7) We used to go to Spain each year and my aunt ___________ always come with us.

8) I took my young _____________ to dog training lessons to teach it to be obedient.

9) He __________ his time at school to gain all the knowledge he could.

10) It was past six o'clock and much__________ than they thought. **Score** 10

Exercise 59b

11) An ________was wearily pulling the plough across the field with a man walking behind.

12) The shop had a __________ to clear all the stock before finally closing down.

13) Sitting at her ___________ in the office, the secretary was typing a letter.

14) "Come over here and look at all _____________ shells that I have collected."

15) When we changed the lock we had to have several copies of the new _________ cut.

16) Teachers help children to ___________ to·read and write.

17) "We can ___________ to the other side here where the stream is narrower."

18) The current was too ____________ and she could not swim against it.

19) She was so forgetful she couldn't __________ remember her son's name.

20) 'A _________ *of Two Cities'* is a famous novel by Charles Dickens. **Score** 10

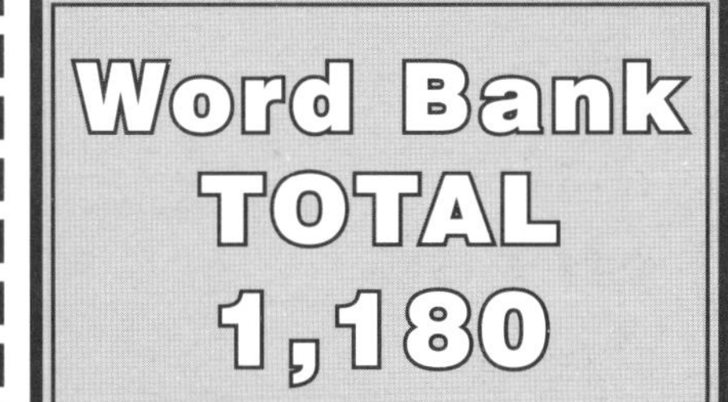

early	**strong**
would	**could**
cross	**these**
those	**thin**

Word Bank TOTAL 1,180

59

Across

1. A story or report that is untrue.
3. Robust and sturdy. Not easily damaged or broken.
6. Angry and upset.
8. Before the expected time.
10. Employ something for some purpose.
12. A time when a shop sell goods at reduced prices.
14. Used when making a polite request or offer.
15. Slim with little body fat.
16. Instrument used for locking and unlocking.
17. Expended or consumed.
18. A table used for work.

Down

2. After the present time.
4. Plural (more than one) of *'that'*.
5. A bovine animal sometimes used for pulling heavy loads and ploughs.
6. Used when making polite requests.
7. Male or female bovine mammals.
9. To come to know something.
11. A dog under a year old.
13. Not sloping, rough, or irregular.
15. Plural (more than one) of *'this'*.

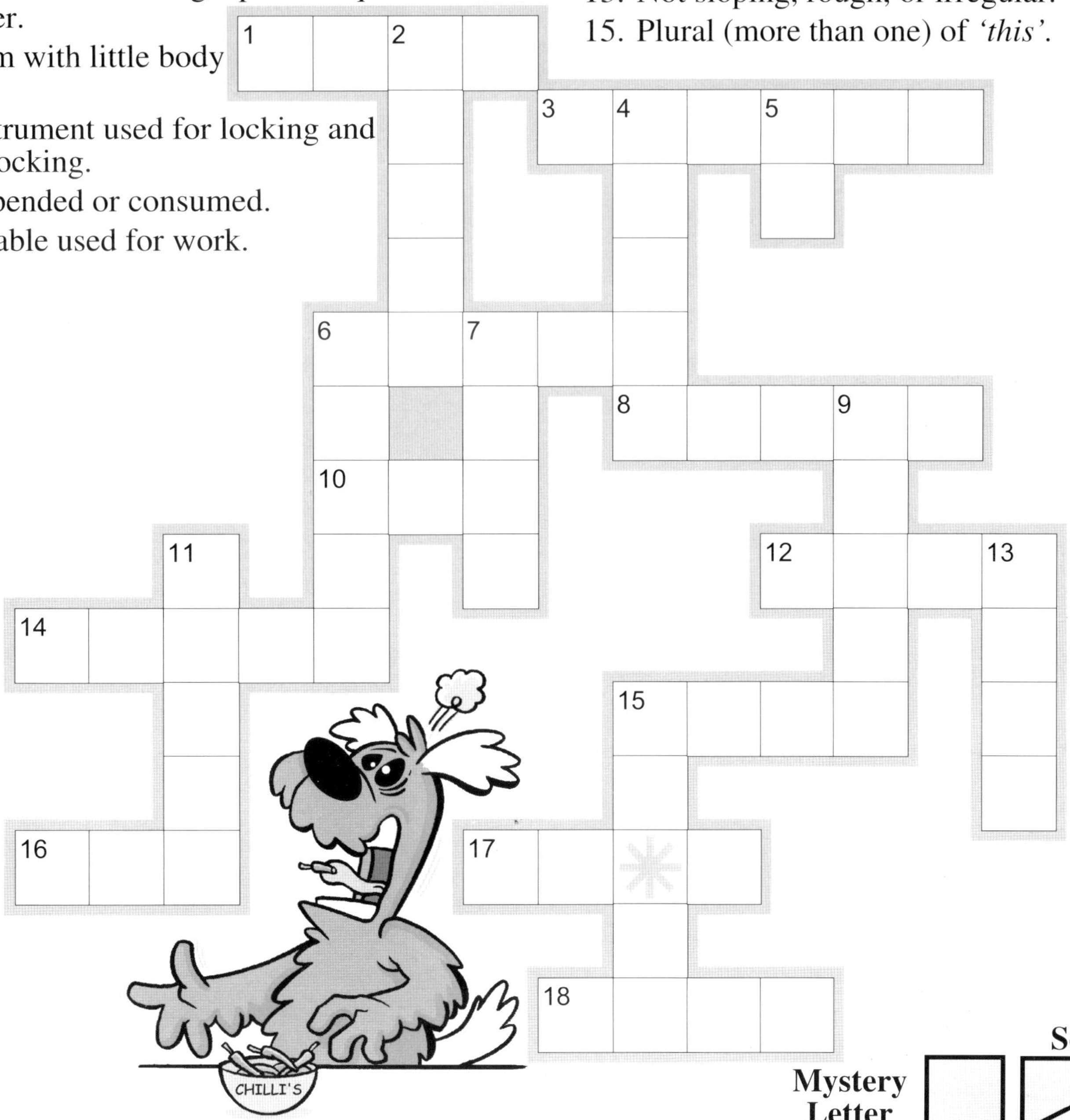

Mystery Letter

Score

/20

Across   **60**

3. Remained.
4. Having the colour of the sky.
6. Showing mental agility and creativity.
8. Following this one.
10. The brother of somebody's mother or father.
12. Something written down as a record or reminder.
13. Finished or completed.
15. Takes action to change a situation or solve a problem.
17. A small piece of rock.
18. Absent after leaving somewhere.

Down

1. Ended their sleep.
2. Took part in a game or sport.
4. Any one of the hard parts forming the skeleton.
5. Unit of length equal to 2.54cm.
7. A tool for measuring and drawing straight lines.
9. Real or correct.
11. Departs.
14. A total or sum.
15. Took somebody somewhere in a vehicle.
16. Complete with nothing left out.

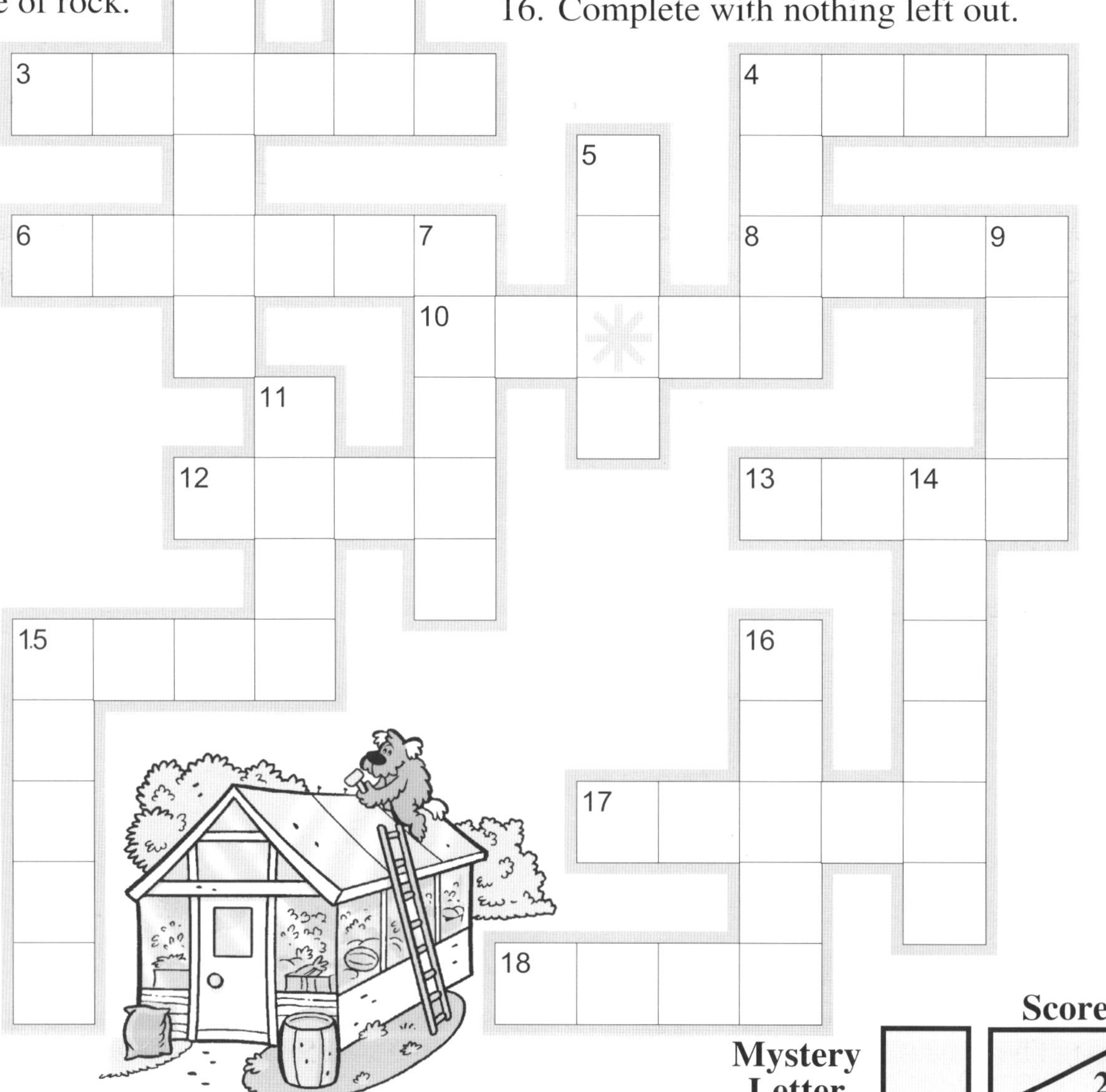

Mystery Letter

Score / 20

Exercise 60a

1) *'The* _____________ *Danube'* is a waltz composed by Johann Straus, the younger.

2) "At what time _____________ your mother usually collect you from school?"

3) The two of them _____________ together nicely until she wouldn't share her toy pram.

4) He missed the eight o'clock train and had to wait for the _____________ one.

5) When the sun _____________ down the evening temperature falls.

6) The imperial measurement of one _____________ is equal to just over 2.5 centimetres.

7) We took a picnic and _____________ the car out into the countryside.

8) She had left a _____________ on the table for her daughter.

9) The note read, " _____________ to the shops - will be back within the hour."

10) That evening he _____________ in and watched the match.

Score / 10

Exercise 60b

11) Although only a few pupils had misbehaved, the _____________ class was punished.

12) Queen Elizabeth I was an able and firm _____________ from 1558 until her death in 1603.

13) He had lied before and now she didn't know if anything he told her was _____________ .

14) After a restless night Sheila _____________ up tired and irritable.

15) All the _____________ used to build St. Paul's Cathedral came from the island of Portland.

16) The femur is the main _____________ in the human thigh and is the strongest in the body.

17) "Let's go to the fair. We haven't _____________ that for years."

18) Albert Einstein was extremely _____________ and a brilliant mathematical physicist.

19) _____________ Arthur was the eldest of my father's brothers.

20) There were a _____________ of options but none was satisfactory.

Score / 10

Exercise 61a

1) She studied the menu and chose _______________________ and cream for dessert.

2) Her wedding dress was made from the finest ____________ .

3) The cowhand worked on the ____________ and slept in the bunkhouse.

4) He always had hot ________________ for breakfast in the winter.

5) His cabin was at the end of a narrow __________________ on the starboard side.

6) She always ______________ his birthday and he has got used to not getting a card.

7) I love the way the skin on his face __________________ when he smiles at me.

8) They had ________________ , beetroot, spring onions and celery in their salad.

9) He was __________________ and taken to the police station to be charged.

10) There was still ______________ food left over for later.

Score 10

Exercise 61b

11) He was a fine _____________ and played many exacting rôles on stage and screen.

12) The ______________ I waited the more convinced I became that he was not coming.

13) He insisted he did not ____________ while asleep but his wife knew differently.

14) I heard a songbird and the ornithologist confirmed it was a ______________ .

15) The __________________ river in the United States of America is the Missouri.

16) We finally ______________ at our destination after an 11 hour journey.

17) The *Titanic* struck an ________________ and sank on her maiden voyage in 1912.

18) I watched the blackbird pull the long ______________ from the soil.

19) The worm continued to ______________ in its beak as the bird flew off.

20) Hirohito was the ________________ of Japan during World War II.

Score 10

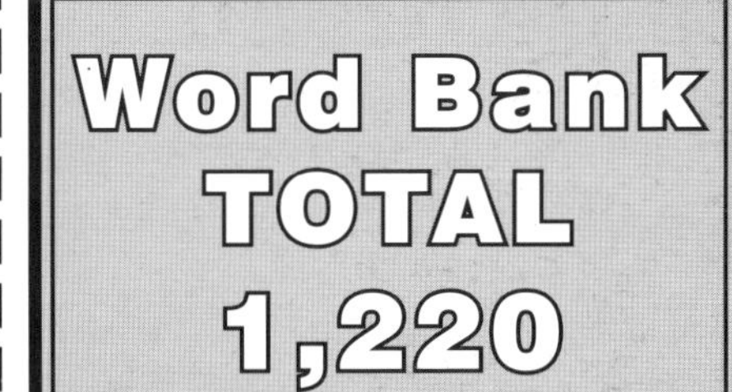

Across — 61

1. Lines or creases in the skin that form on the face.
4. To breathe noisily when asleep.
6. A little or quite a few.
8. A livestock farm on open land in North and South America and Australia.
10. A performer in plays on stage, in films and on television.
12. With a greater length.
13. The ruler of an empire.
14. The thread from silkworms and fabric made from it.
16. To twist and turn.
17. An invertebrate with a slender, soft, cylindrical or flat body.
18. Hot breakfast cereal made from oatmeal.

Down

1. Stopped, or taken into custody.
3. A passage inside a building.
5. A plant with edible leaves usually eaten in salads.
7. Does not remember.
9. A small songbird.
10. Reached a place having come from another place.
11. Edible heart-shaped red fruit.
12. With the greatest length.
15. A mass of ice floating in the sea.

Mystery Letter   **Score**

20

! Don't forget to go back to page 21 and
● complete **Dicken's Mystery Word.**

In the Countryside

bridge	stile	mole	ramblers	retriever
fox	flask	badger	wood	rabbit
windmill	footpath	deer	kestrel	stream

1.____________________ 2.____________________ 3.____________________

4.____________________ 5.____________________ 6.____________________

7.____________________ 8.____________________ 9.____________________

10.____________________ 11.____________________ 12.____________________

13.____________________ 14.____________________ 15.____________________

In the High Street

Can you find all these words in the picture below? Write in the correct word against each number as you find them.

streetlight	**lorry**	**drain**	**butcher**	**road works**
newsagent	**pushcair**	**kerb**	**ironmonger**	**crossing**
greengrocer	**florist**	**bank**	**carrier bag**	**supermarket**

1.______________________ 2.______________________ 3.______________________

4.______________________ 5.______________________ 6.______________________

7.______________________ 8.______________________ 9.______________________

10._____________________ 11._____________________ 12._____________________

13._____________________ 14._____________________ 15._____________________

Exercise 62a

1) His favourite _____________________ programme would be broadcast at 8.00 p.m.

2) "The performance is about to commence. Would you ____________ take your seats."

3) The audience were all looking upwards to see the exciting ______________ act.

4) He carried his _____________________ over his arm in case it rained.

5) He drove along the road ________________ searching for the correct address.

6) The postman knocked _____________ but no one came to the door.

7) He was the ______________ in the class and rose head and shoulders above the rest.

8) The circus ______________ kept seven clubs in the air at once.

9) Details of their homework were written on the _________________________ .

10) He _____________ the rugby ball into touch and the game ended.　**Score** /10

Exercise 62b

11) It all happened so ___________________ that it took them by surprise.

12) She was wearing new shoes and they were beginning to _____________ her toes.

13) It was their golden wedding anniversary - 50 years of being _____________ married.

14) The Bolshoi _____________ company performed *Swan Lak*e in Moscow.

15) "Answer this question ______________ . Have you looked at the answers?"

16) The groundsman used the heavy _____________ to flatten the wicket.

17) My hamster is ________________ Krusty after the clown in the *Simpsons*.

18) We were entertained by a very skilful ______________ 's gymnastic display.

19) His dinner _____________ was stained and had to be dry-cleaned.

20) "Put everything back ____________ and in the right place."　**Score** /10

Across

62

3. A video broadcasting system.
5. A large heavy device for flattening lawns.
7. To grip or squeeze something between finger and thumb.
10. Neatly and methodically.
12. A short coat.
13. Joyfully, contentedly, or willingly.
17. Said something in a loud voice.
18. The highest of them all.
19. Fairly or justly, truthfully or genuinely.
20. A horizontal bar between two hanging ropes often used in a circus.

Down

1. Struck with the foot.
2. Not moving quickly.
4. A gymnastic entertainer.
6. Friendly and generous by nature.
8. A raincoat originally made from rubberized fabric.
9. A board of dark colour that is written on with chalk.
11. Noisily.
14. Happening quickly and unexpectedly.
15. A person who can keep several objects in motion in the air at the same time.
16. A form of dance with graceful movements.

Score

/ 20

Put the mystery letter (✳) into box **62** below. Add in the starred letters from puzzles **63** to **69** then rearrange them to make **Oliver's Mystery Word**.

The clue is **MINERAL**

62	63	64	65	66	67	68	69

Enter your mystery letters here:

Now rearrange them:

Mystery Word:

Across   **63**   ## Down

Across

5. Growled loudly.
6. Puts clothes on.
8. Feeling afraid.
10. Having been on many journeys.
11. Hitting hands together quickly and loudly
13. Become or make sharp or sharper.
15. Using little pressure.
17. Container for clothes and other belongings during travel.
18. Making little noise.
19. Spoke to God or some other being.
20. Fabric bag for sleeping in when camping.

Down

1. Loose waterproof rubber boots.
2. Framework for carrying things on the roof of a vehicle.
3. An amount that can be held in the hand.
4. Mobile home designed for towing.
7. Unhappily.
9. Went in.
12. In a inferior or inadequate way.
14. Attached or held firmly.
16. Concentrated on hearing.

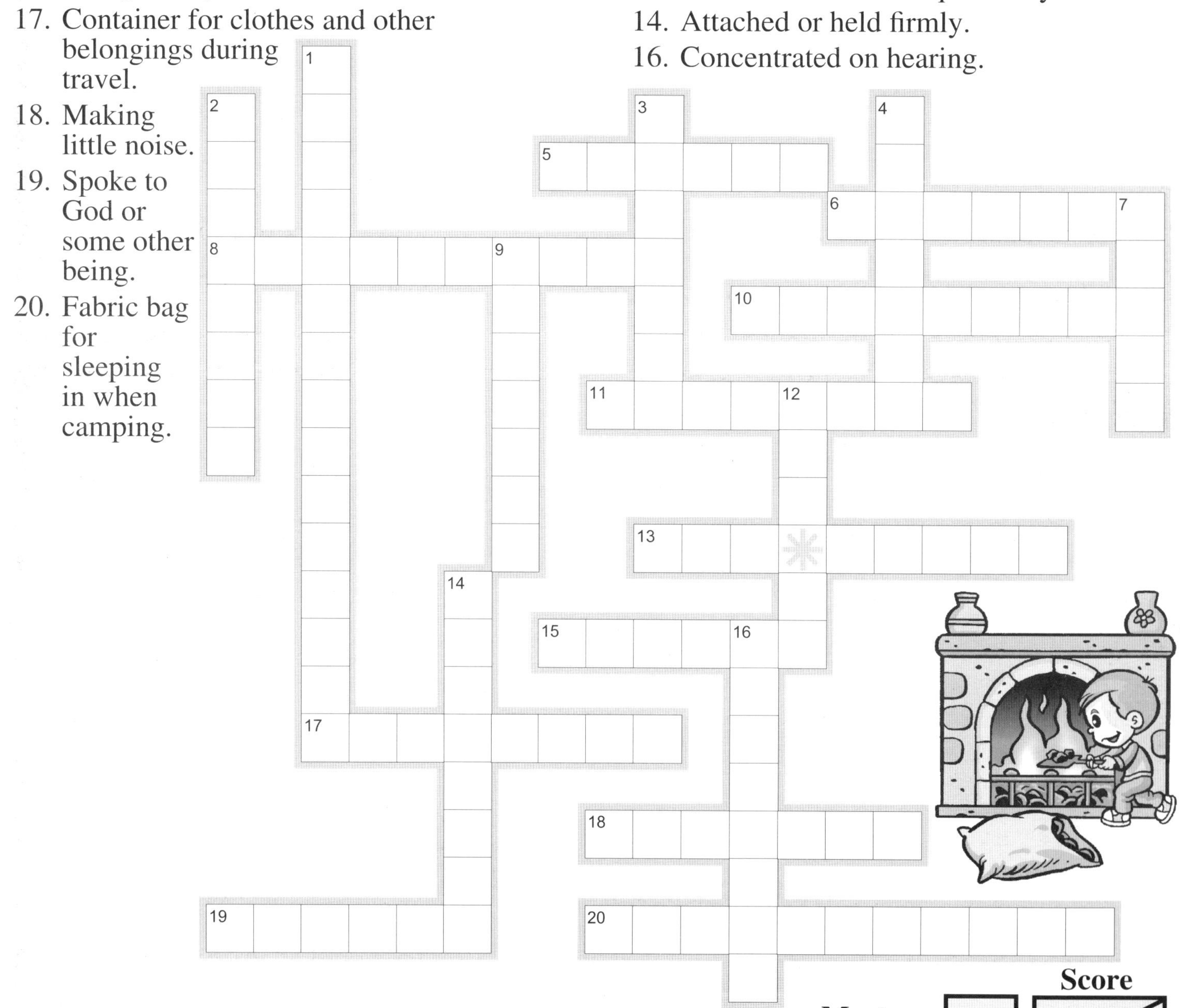

Mystery Letter

Score / 20

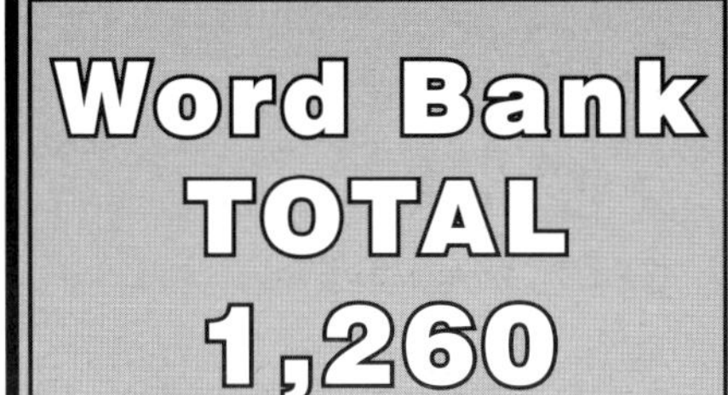

Exercise 63a

1) It was locked securely with a heavy chain _________________ with large padlock.

2) The monitor had _________________ all the pencils in the art room.

3) Last year we stayed in a _________________ on a site in the south of France.

4) "Don't be _________________ it won't hurt you."

5) The robber _________________ the shop and demanded money.

6) I had hoped to see her before she left but ____________ it wasn't to be.

7) They had _________________ a long way and they needed to refuel the car.

8) Only a _______________ of volunteers turned up to help unload the lorries.

9) The nurse removed the bandages very ______________ to avoid hurting him.

10) He felt very ____________ and went to bed with a hot water bottle. **Score** | 10

Exercise 63b

11) "Please open your _________________ for inspection," demanded the customs officer.

12) The lion was annoyed and ______________ loudly to show its displeasure.

13) "Take off your muddy ______________________ before you come in."

14) The entire audience were on their feet and _________________ in appreciation.

15) In the morning she turned her _________________ inside out and hung it up to air.

16) The car was very heavily loaded - even the _________________ had suitcases on it.

17) "It's very late. Please be considerate and leave ______________ ."

18) She had put out her washing that morning and she ______________ it would not rain.

19) He lay awake and _______________ to the waves crashing onto the rocks.

20) "I have come to collect the _______________ for the bridesmaids." **Score** | 10

Exercise 64a

1) The prize __________ was a magnificent beast and won first prize at the county show.

2) The circus __________________ wore a red jacket, white breeches and black boots.

3) They started to modernize the house by installing a new bathroom ____________.

4) "Would you like ____________ or biscuits with your cheese, madam?"

5) It was his ambition to conduct an ________________ playing at the Albert Hall.

6) "Get onto the ____________ and we'll see if you've lost any weight."

7) I expect she was as ________________ as I was that we missed each other.

8) They built a splendid ________________ then watched the waves demolish it.

9) She pulled off every ______________ from the flower until none was left.

10) The wind changed direction suddenly and the __________ capsized. **Score** / 10

Exercise 64b

11) "Go to the the back of the ______________ and wait your turn like everyone else!"

12) Whilst on safari our group was fortunate to see a ______________ sleeping in the shade.

13) He had many ambitions but his main __________ was to be a professional footballer.

14) Rabbits were ________________ away from the cycle track as we approched them.

15) Their music was very good and the ________________ beat out a steady rhythm.

16) She put the ice cubes into a polythene bag and used a ________________ to crush it.

17) "Golden Delicious are my favourite ______________ but mum prefers Coxes."

18) They had to protect their sandwiches from a ______________ that swooped down.

19) We dug a large __________ in the garden and fittted the new pond into it.

20) His eyes were tired and he kept ____________ them with his hand. **Score** / 10

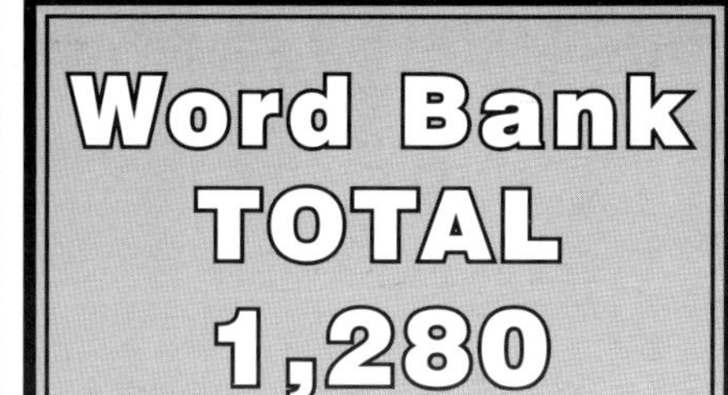

seagull
hole
ringmaster
rolling-pin
goal
drummer
rubbing
scales

Word Bank TOTAL 1,280

64

Across

3. Sailing boat.
5. Not satisfied.
7. Large spotted African cat.
12. A web-footed white-and-grey sea bird.
13. Large group of musicians.
14. Climbs up a steep incline.
16. A model castle made of damp sand.
17. A kitchen utensil used for rolling out dough and pastry.
19. A hollow space in a solid object.

Down

1. Pressing and moving the hand over the surface of something.
2. Line of people or vehicles waiting.
4. Plural (more than one) of apple.
6. Somebody who plays the drums.
8. Somebody who announces acts and events at a circus.
9. Long-stemmed vegetable with crisp, flattish stems often eaten raw.
10. One of the coloured parts of a flower.
11. Jumping lightly on one foot.
15. Adult male of domestic cattle or other bovine animal.
16. Set of matching furniture.
18. Opening into which a ball or puck must go to score points.

Mystery Letter

Score

20

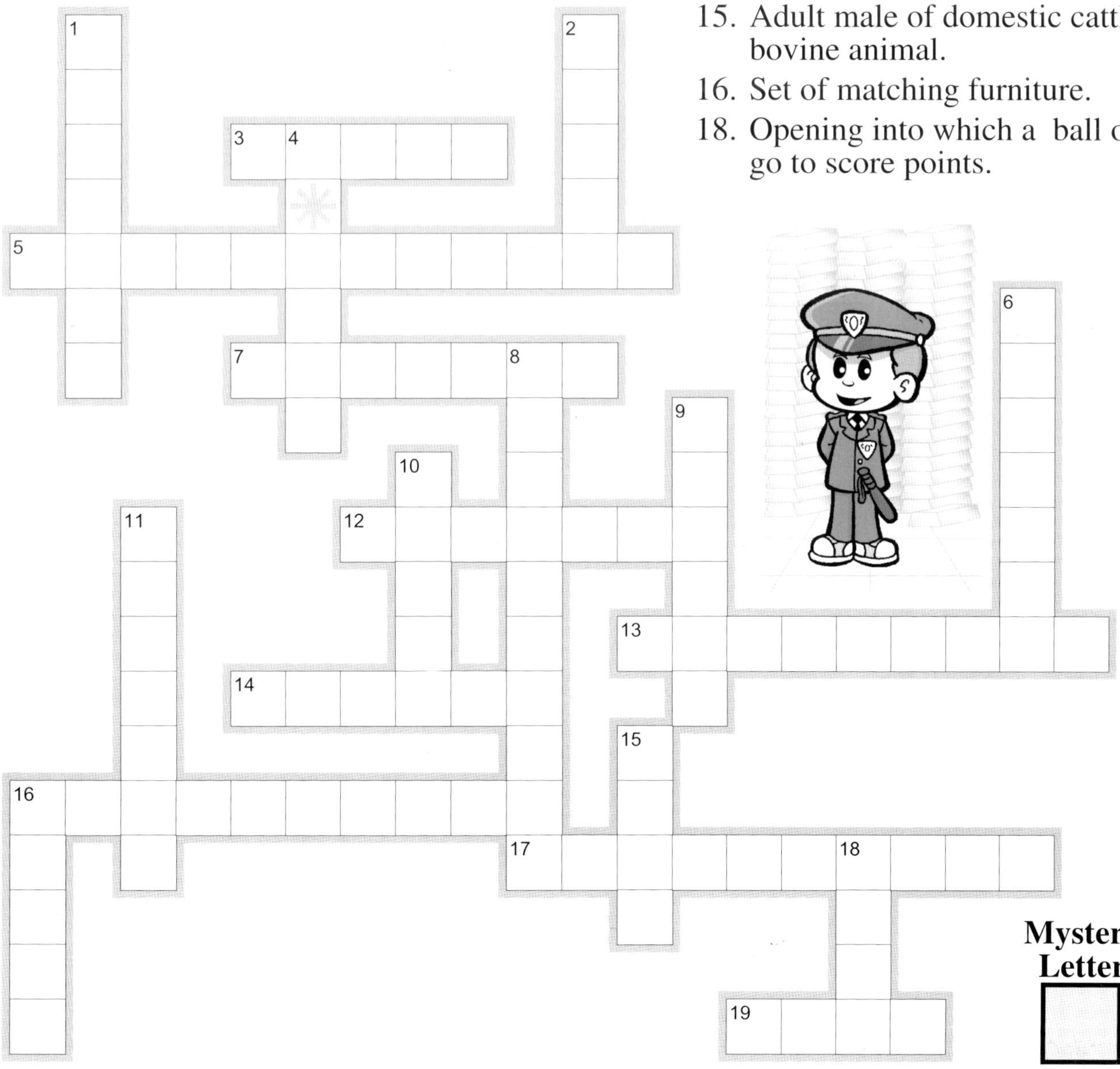

Across

65

4. To take small quick bites.
5. Things to play with.
8. Hard-backed insect.
10. A large wading bird with long legs.
13. An object for scaring birds away.
15. Resembles or looks like.
19. Knowing something.
20. A shallow pool of water.

Down

1. Somebody who serves at tables.
2. Somebody who installs and repairs water or drainage pipes and fixtures.
3. A place where goods are kept.
6. To cuddle up.
7. Clothing worn for swimming.
9. Lengths of thread to join or decorate material.
11. Showing concern for others.
12. Aircraft designed to carry and drop bombs.
14. Covered up with paper or cloth.
16. Pieces of metal money.
17. Becomes or makes opaque or murky.
18. To walk with short steps causing the body to tilt slightly from side to side.

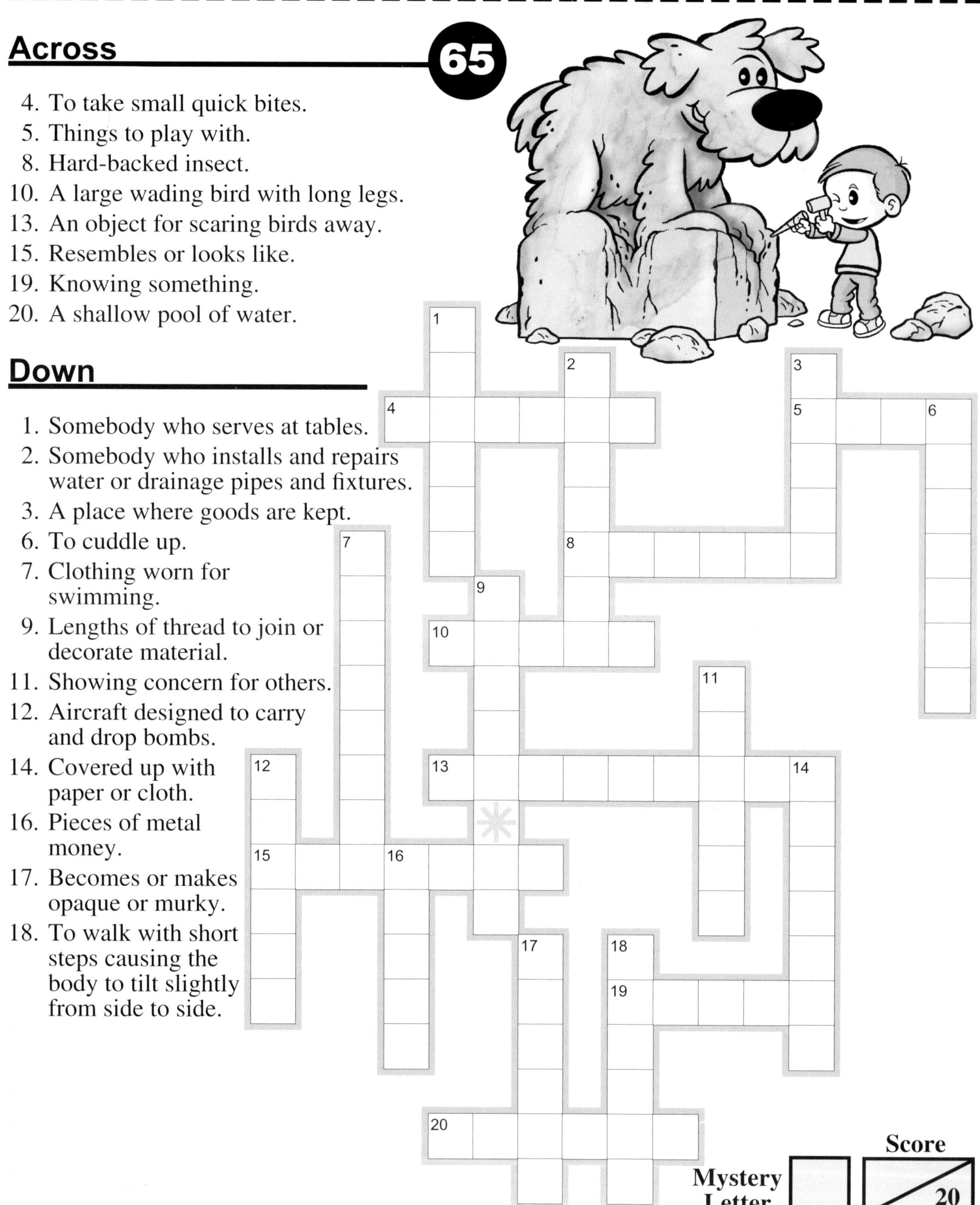

Mystery Letter

Score

20

Exercise 65a

1) "Don't let your little brother play with _________________ . He could start a fire."

2) She changed into her _________________ before going to paddle in the sea.

3) The squirrel held the nut in his paws and started to _____________ it.

4) Her purse was full of change and the _______________ were very heavy.

5) The cut was very deep and it needed seven _________________ before being dressed.

6) The sandwiches were _________________ in silver foil to keep them fresh.

7) Large black _______________ were gathering overhead and it looked like rain.

8) In the field the _________________ was protecting the crops from the birds.

9) A stag ________________ 's long extended jaws are called mandibles.

10) The _________________ was shot down but the aircrew survived. **Score** / 10

Exercise 65b

11) My dad called the _________________ when we had a burst pipe last winter.

12) "Pull up the covers, _________________ down in your bed and keep warm.

13) At the zoo we saw a ___________ with a long, straight bill standing on one leg.

14) He didn't so much walk as _________________ like a duck along the pavement.

15) My dad uses old jam jars to ________________ nails and screws on a shelf in the shed.

16) He had a summer job working as a ________________ in the town's finest restaurant.

17) She was _________________ of someone behind her and turned to see who it was.

18) It was a very deep ________________ and the water came over the top of his boots.

19) "Play nicely together and share your ___________ with your friends."

20) The paramedics were ________________ for the injured passengers. **Score** / 10

Exercise 66a

1) The bear bared his teeth and began to ____________ angrily.

2) It was very dark in the __________ between the buildings and dustbins lined the sides.

3) He used his ____________ to breathe through as he swam face down in the sea.

4) Her feet were ____________ with the cold and she wished she had worn her boots.

5) The racehorse fell at the last fence and its ______________ was unseated.

6) She was late and had to ________________ back indoors without being heard.

7) Every Wednesday evening they played a few frames of ________________ together.

8) The hexagonal paving slabs looked like __________________ when they were laid.

9) Pollyanna wore petticoats and long, frilly ________________ under her skirt.

10) That evening the ____________ had given birth to a foal.

Score / 10

Exercise 66b

11) The terrorists planted a ______________ hidden in holdall but it was defused safely.

12) "Try turning the __________ and see if the door will open."

13) My granddad closed his eyes and had a short ________________ after Sunday lunch.

14) The doe lifted her nose to ____________ the air in order to detect a preditor.

15) Their __________________ had stones for his eyes and mouth and a carrot for a nose.

16) A huge pig had his ______________ deep in the trough and was eating noisily.

17) He went into hospital to have an operation to remove a ________________ stone.

18) She had a small ______________ to keep her going until dinner time.

19) "Use this small __________ of material to patch the hole.

20) "Cover your nose if you think you are going to ____________ ."

Score / 10

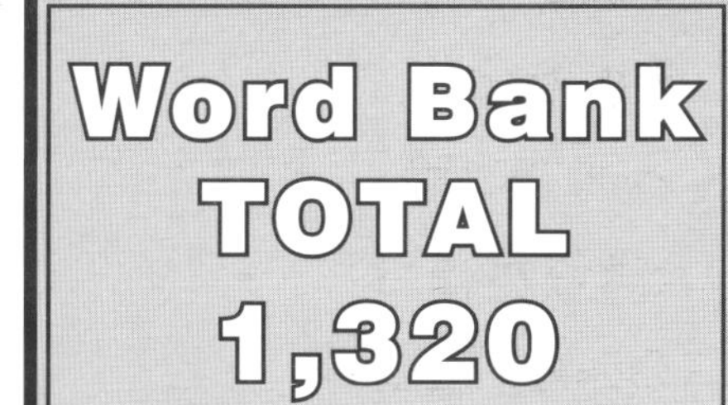

Across

66

3. Breathing apparatus for swimming just below water.
6. An organ in the abdomen that filters waste liquid.
7. To have a short sleep or nap.
8. With no feeling or sensation.
10. A rider of racehorses.
14. A roughly human figure made from snow.
15. A rounded handle or dial.
16. Adult female horse.
17. To go or act in a stealthy, secretive way.
18. Growl threateningly.
19. To breathe in through the nose.

Down

1. Game played with balls and a cue.
2. A small or narrrow street.
4. An animal's nose.
5. A wax structure made of hexagonal (six-sided) cells made by bees.

Down (Continued)

9. A missile containing explosive or other destructive material.
11. Panties worn by women and girls.
12. A sudden involuntary expulsion of air through the nose.
13. To cut using small strokes.
17. Small meal.

Mystery Letter

Score

/20

45

Across

67

2. A large amount of money or possessions.
4. Utter a roar like a bull.
5. A small European snake with black zigzag pattern on its back.
9. Edible North Atlantic fish related to but smaller than the cod.
12. An aggressive person who mistreats weaker people.
14. Decayed.
15. An aquatic fish-eating mammal with smooth dark brown fur and webbed feet.
16. A seabird that cannot fly.
17. Somebody who climbs rocks or mountains.
19. A bowl-shaped fixture for disposing of bodily waste.
20. A vagrant who has no home and travels on foot.

Down (Continued)

10. To travel by sea on a pleasure trip.
11. A grave or burial chamber
13. A woodworker in the building trade.
18. Slightly wet or damp.

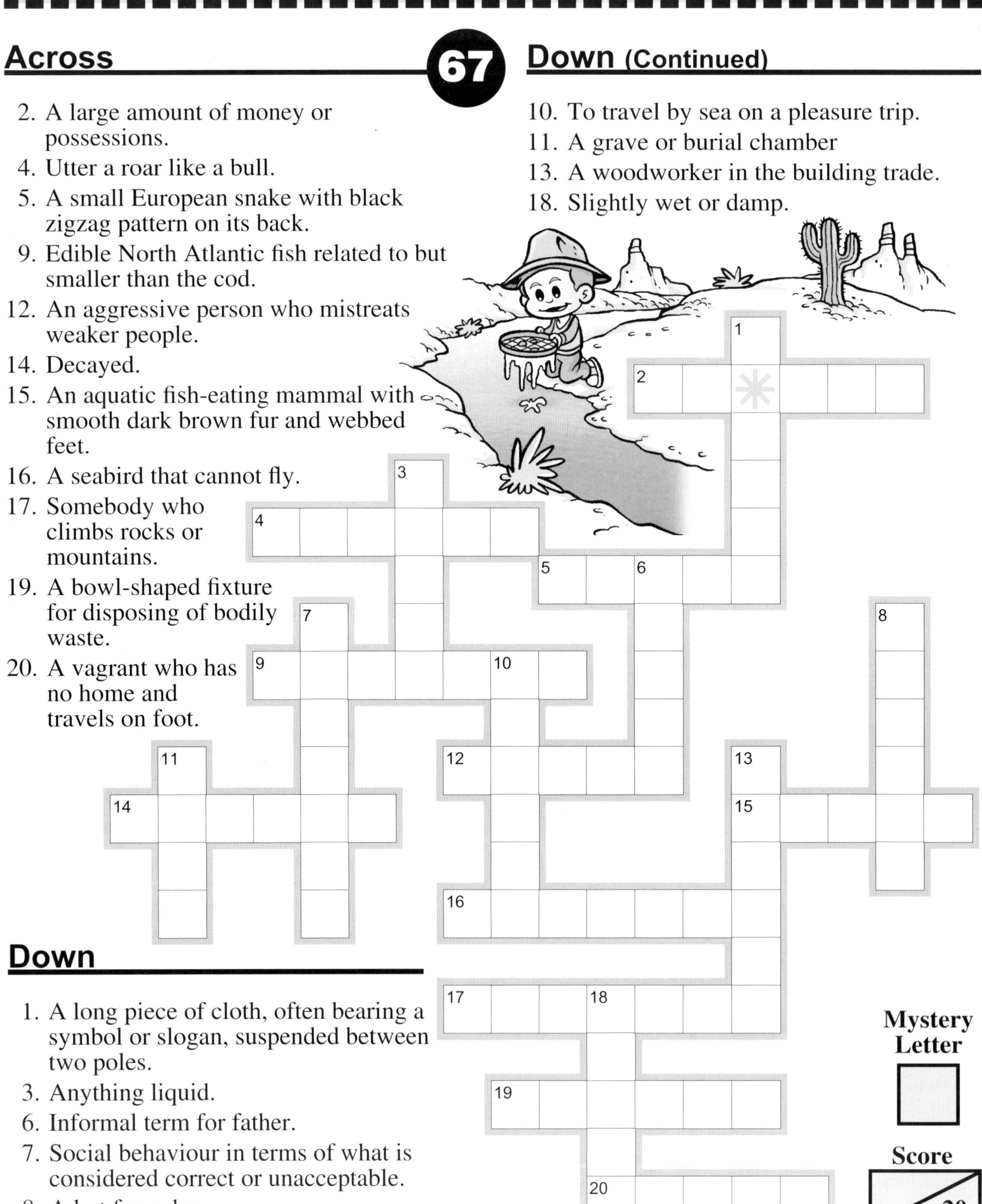

Down

1. A long piece of cloth, often bearing a symbol or slogan, suspended between two poles.
3. Anything liquid.
6. Informal term for father.
7. Social behaviour in terms of what is considered correct or unacceptable.
8. A hut for a dog.

Mystery Letter

Score

20

Exercise 67a

1) He slipped because the grass was still _____________ from the earlier rainfall.

2) He was roped on so when he lost his footing the _____________ did not fall.

3) They unfurled a long _____________ and draped it across the front of the building.

4) The _____________ is the only snake in Britain with a poisonous bite.

5) In the pharaoh's _____________ were many valuable treasures to be excavated.

6) He was a man of great _____________ with many assets and several properties.

7) Every night my _____________ reads my little sister a story before bedtime.

8) From the barn could be heard a loud _____________ from the bull.

9) New door frames and window frames were made by the _____________ .

10) He built a new _____________ for his dog when the old one leaked. **Score** [/ 10]

Exercise 67b

11) I love to watch the _____________ catching fish that the zookeeper throws to it.

12) "Don't be a _____________ Martin, pick on someone your own size!"

13) Mum had cod and chips for super but dad had _____________ with his chips.

14) The _____________ ship called at another port on its voyage around the Mediterranean.

15) It is good _____________ to stand back and let others go first.

16) "Would you please put some bleach down the _____________ to disinfect it?"

17) Bleach is a very viscous _____________ that clings to the inside of the toilet bowl.

18) In its mouth the _____________ held a large salmon that it had caught.

19) The floor joists were _____________ and had to be replaced.

20) "Don't _____________ all over the flower bed, I've just hoed it!" **Score** [/ 10]

Exercise 68a

1) She felt a ______________ of hunger and realized she had not eaten for several hours.

2) The ____________ driver had braked on the wet road and his vehicle had jackknifed.

3) "What's your ____________ ? I spend my spare time collecting ancient coins."

4) The new tree was not very sturdy so the gardener used a stake to ____________ it up.

5) She stood on the windy promenade and could feel the salty ____________ on her face.

6) In the ____________ was her new baby and they were out for a walk for the first time.

7) At the station the porter used a ______________ to carry their cases to the train.

8) "You'll feel a slight ___________ ," said the nurse before she gave him the injection.

9) A solitary pale yellow __________________ was growing in the rockery.

10) The wind got up and began to _______________ her long hair.

Score [/ 10]

Exercise 68b

11) He had bought a new locomotive for his ______________ railway set.

12) I went to the late night _________________ to get some cough mixture.

13) His _______________ task was to find some wood so that he could light a fire.

14) _______________ the fender over the boat's side he slipped and fell into the river.

15) The fairy lights made the ______________ on the Christmas tree sparkle.

16) *Do not stop on the ______________ crossing'*, said the warning sign.

17) On their cycling holiday they spent the nights at a youth _____________ .

18) When _________________ of the USA, Abraham Lincoln was assassinated in 1865.

19) She was often on all fours __________________ the wooden floors.

20) We took our car to Ireland on the ____________ .

Score [/ 10]

Across

68

2. Cleaning by rubbing hard.
4. An enjoyable activity for pleasure and relaxation.
6. To puncture and make a small hole through the surface.
7. Accommodation for homeless people.
11. A rigid beam, stake, or pole that supports something.
15. To tangle or fray.
16. The first in a sequence or ranked as most important.
17. A copy of an object usually made on a smaller scale.
18. The head of a state or republic.
19. A boat making regular short river or sea crossings.

Down

1. A jet of fine liquid particles.
3. A shop selling medicines and toiletries.
5. A two-wheeled hand cart.
8. A thin strip of glittering material.
9. Large road vehicle for transporting goods.
10. Not sloping.
12. A spring plant with pale yellow flowers.
13. Throwing violently.
14. A small wheeled vehicle for carrying babies.
16. A short sharp pain.

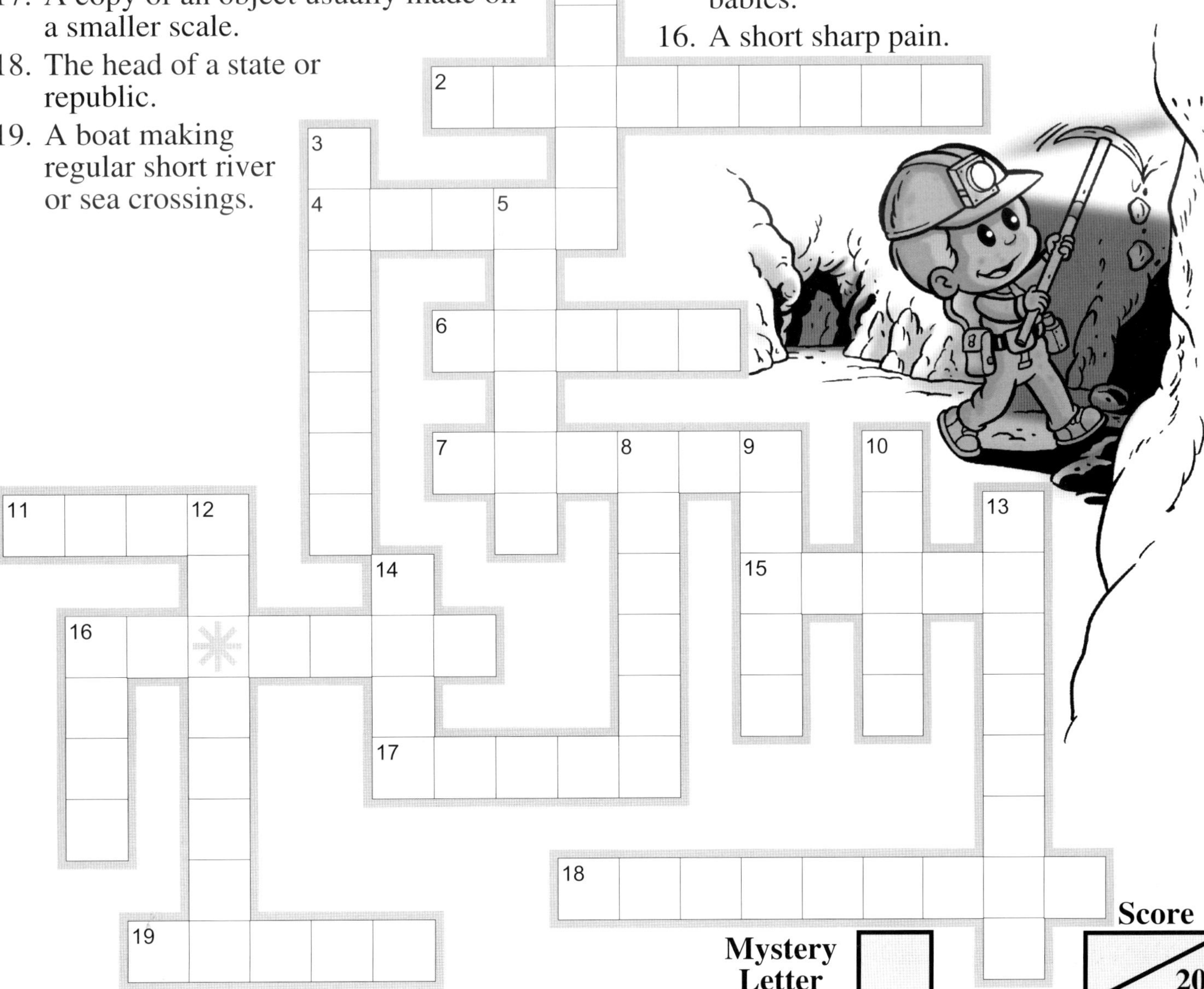

Mystery Letter

Score /20

49

Across

69

2. To make beer.
4. Breathes long and loud in relief or weariness.
5. To move.
7. Wet material, especially watery snow.
10. One less than 20.
11. Felt a need or desire for something.
13. Pretending to be shy.
14. A jumbled mass of fibres or lines.
15. A rigid bracelet.
16. One more than seventeen.
17. Ten add seven.
18. The soya bean plant.

Down

1. Causing fear or alarm.
3. Damaging or ruining something.
4. The number 70.

Down (Continued)

6. A dish of meat, fish, or vegetables cooked by slow simmering.
8. A narrow shelf against the wall.
9. A cabinet with shelves for storing books.
12. To succeed in doing or gaining something.
14. A sheer, one-piece, close-fitting garment covering the body from waist to feet.

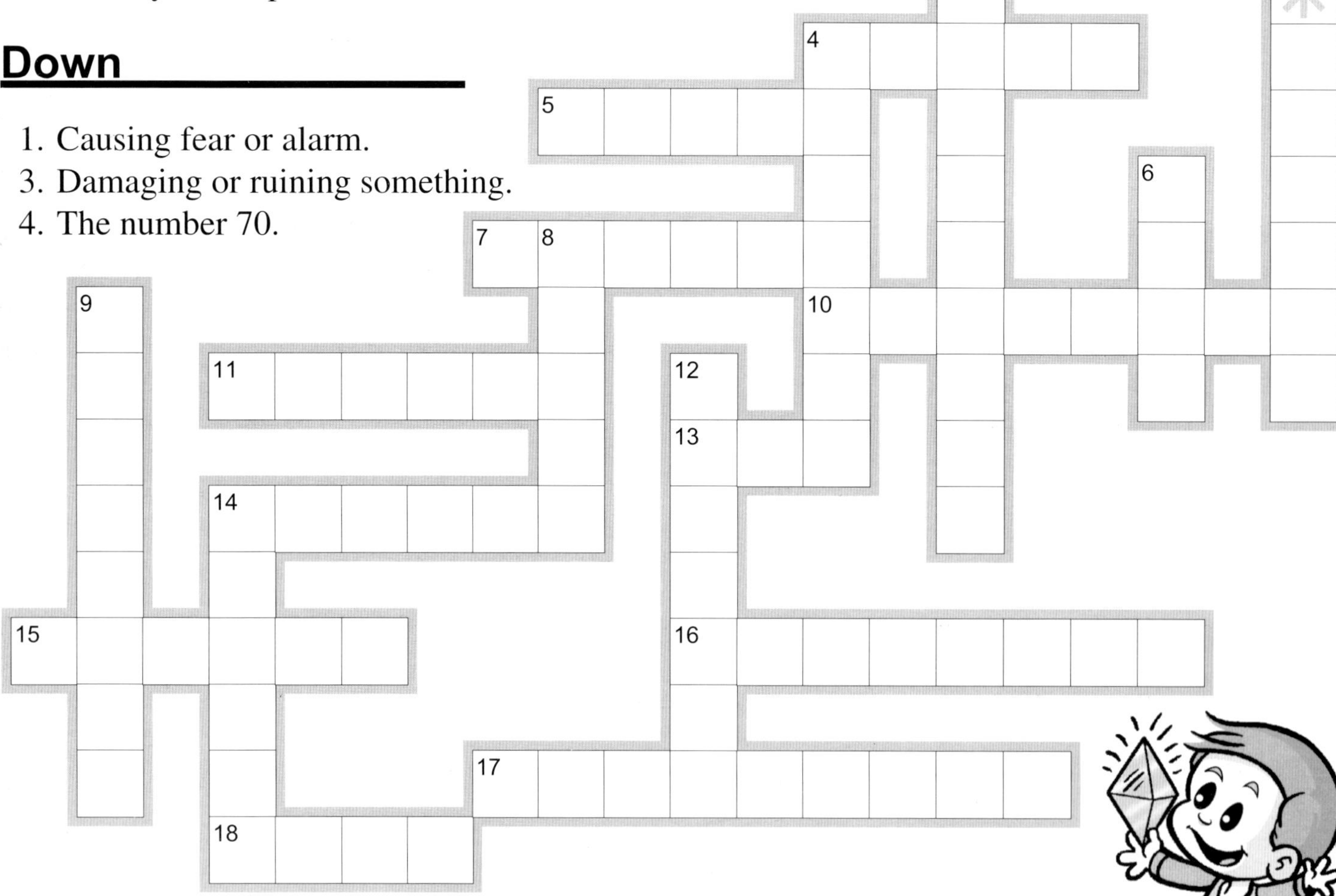

! Don't forget to go back to page **37** and complete **Oliver's Mystery Word.**

Mystery Letter

Score

20

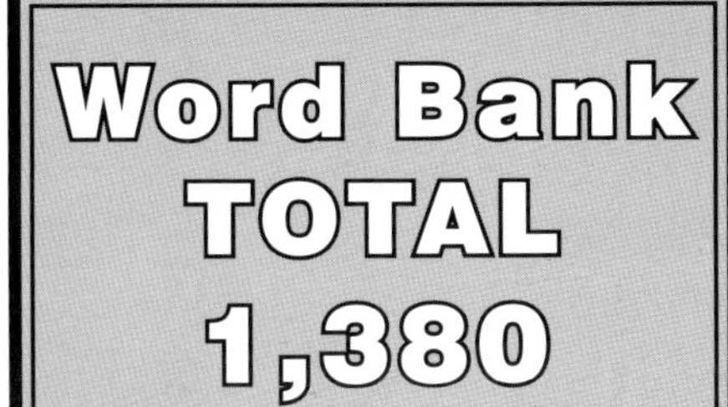

Exercise 69a

1) Being born at the beginning of the 20th century he was ______________ in 1970.

2) She had made a steaming hot Irish __________ with meat and vegetables.

3) There were encyclopaedias, a dictionary and a thesaurus in the ________________ .

4) Soy sauce is dark and salty and made by fermenting __________ beans in brine.

5) You have to be over ______________ to vote in a local or general election.

6) It was a very ____________________ experience and she had nightmares afterwards.

7) The sounds made by the wind as it blew through the trees were like eerie __________ .

8) "Make sure the cat doesn't ____________ my wool while I make myself a cup of tea."

9) "Come away and stop ______________ their fun by annoying them."

10) She had to be __________________ to drive a car for the first time. **Score** / **10**

Exercise 69b

11) She was teasing him by being _________ and pretending to be shy.

12) He tried with all his might to move it but it just would not ______________ .

13) She had seen ______________ different species of bird. One more would make twenty.

14) "Let the tea __________ for a couple of minutes to bring out the full flavour."

15) The acrobat wore a white singlet, white _____________ and white slippers.

16) The drain was partially blocked with a thick _____________ and had to be cleaned out.

17) She slipped the solid gold _____________ over her hand and pushed it up her arm.

18) He desperately_________________ to go with them but his mother would not let him.

19) They were stuck on a rocky ____________ and had to wait to be rescued.

20) I helped him to ______________ success but he took all the credit. **Score** / **10**

51

Book Three Word List

achieve	blame	cried	felt
acrobat	bless	cries	ferry
actor	blew	cross	few
adder	blue	crow	filled
air	boil	cruise	finch
alive	bomb	crying	firm
alley	bomber	curl	flat
along	bone	daddy	flies
any	bookcase	dance	flinging
anything	bound	dead	flower
apples	bow	death	fluid
arrested	brew	desk	follow
arrived	bright	dew	food
asked	broom	die	football
aware	brown	died	forget
babies	budge	dirt	forgets
ballet	bull	disappointed	fork
bangle	bully	doctor	fresh
banner	bunch	does	frightened
barn	burn	done	frightening
barrow	called	downstairs	garden
basket	caravan	draw	gay
bath	card	dream	gently
beach	caring	dresses	getting
beads	carried	drew	giving
bean	carry	drill	glass
beast	celery	dropped	goal
beat	chemist	dropping	goat
became	cherries	drove	goes
bedroom	cherry	drummer	gone
beetle	church	early	great
before	clapping	east	green
behind	class	easy	grew
bellow	clear	eighteen	haddock
belong	clever	emperor	handful
below	climber	entered	happily
belt	cloud	even	harm
berries	clouds	fail	having
berry	coins	farm	heard
beside	cool	farmer	heat
better	corridor	fastened	heel
bigger	could	fear	hobby
biggest	coy	feast	hole
blackboard	cream	feel	honestly

Book Three Word List

honeycomb	longest	orchestra	reading
hopping	looked	otter	ready
hostel	looking	outside	rice
hour	lorry	own	riding
hurt	loud	ox	right
iceberg	loudly	oxen	ringmaster
inch	low	pail	roared
inside	mackintosh	pair	roller
jacket	maid	pang	rolling-pin
jelly	manners	party	roof-rack
jockey	many	pass	rotten
join	march	paw	row
joiner	mare	pence	rubbing
jolly	marry	penguin	ruler
juggler	master	petal	running
kennel	matches	pie	sadly
kept	meal	pinch	sail
key	mean	pink	sale
kicked	meat	played	sand-castle
kidney	melt	playground	scales
kindly	merry	please	scarecrow
knew	mice	plumber	scrubbing
knickers	mix	point	seagull
knob	model	pool	seen
know	moist	poorly	seventeen
ladies	nail	pork	seventy
lame	neat	porridge	shade
later	new	pound	shall
lead	next	pram	shame
leaf	nibble	prayed	sharp
lean	night	president	sharpened
learn	nineteen	press	shirt
least	nor	prick	sighs
ledge	north	primary	silk
leopard	note	primrose	sir
less	nothing	prop	skipping
lettuce	numb	puddle	sleeping-bag
level	number	puppy	slippers
lie	oak	queue	slow
lies	off	quietly	slowly
listened	oil	ranch	sludge
living	once	ravel	snack
load	opened	raw	snarl
longer	opening	reach	sneak

Book Three Word List

sneeze	stitches	third	waddle
sniff	stone	those	waiter
snip	stopped	throw	walked
snooker	store	tidily	walking
snooze	stories	tights	wanted
snore	stork	tinsel	warm
snorkel	strawberries	tiny	washed
snout	strong	toilet	wealth
snowman	such	tomb	wellington boots
snuggle	suck	tomorrow	which
some	suddenly	tonight	whip
sound	suitcase	tooth	who
south	suite	town	whole
soya	swimsuit	toys	why
spade	tale	tramp	window
speak	talked	trapeze	within
speaking	talking	travelled	without
spell	tallest	tried	woke
spelling	tame	tries	word
spill	tangle	trip	world
spoiling	teeth	true	worm
spray	television	turn	would
stair	their	two	wrapped
star	these	uncle	wriggle
start	thin	upstairs	wrinkles
stayed	think	use	yacht
stew	thinking	used	yard

Congratulations!

You have now learnt to spell **1,380** words; know what they mean and how to use them in a sentence.

Now move on to **Book 4** to learn lots more words to add to your word bank total.

Answers

Exercise 47a
1) farm
2) such
3) bedroom
4) harm
5) shade
6) heat
7) neat
8) garden
9) beat
10) Bless

Exercise 47b
11) less
12) window
13) Press
14) farmer
15) card
16) yard
17) barn
18) broom
19) meat
20) spade

Crossword No. 47

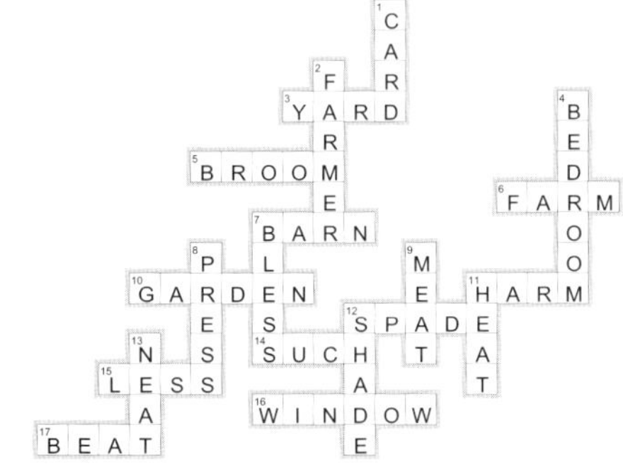

Letter = T

Exercise 48a
1) fear
2) *beast*
3) bunch
4) brown
5) pink
6) glass
7) heard
8) pass
9) clear
10) leaf

Exercise 48b
11) class
12) east
13) town
14) belt
15) flat
16) flower
17) sail
18) think
19) feast
20) pail

Crossword No. 48

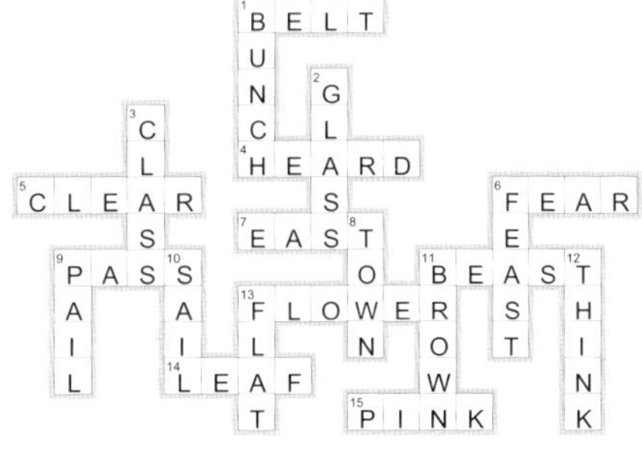

Letter = A

Exercise 49a
1) lame
2) spelling
3) drill
4) dream
5) pie
6) tame
7) fail
8) least
9) spill
10) blame

Exercise 49b
11) die
12) shame
13) nail
14) cream
15) meal
16) spell
17) lie
18) pool
19) suck
20) mix

Crossword No. 49

Letter = E

Answers

Exercise 50a

1) death
2) sir
3) oak
4) burn
5) dead
6) ready
7) church
8) third
9) cool
10) shirt

Exercise 50b

11) load
12) goat
13) dirt
14) curl
15) lies
16) Turn
17) firm
18) died
19) hurt
20) food

Crossword No. 50

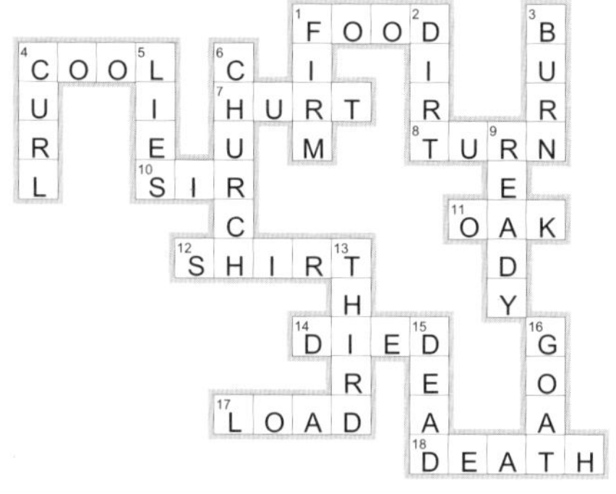

Letter = H

Exercise 51a

1) crow
2) star
3) upstairs
4) low
5) inside
6) night
7) pair
8) forget
9) slow
10) start

Exercise 51b

11) tonight
12) outside
13) stair
14) word
15) downstairs
16) right
17) air
18) world
19) within
20) bright

Crossword No. 51

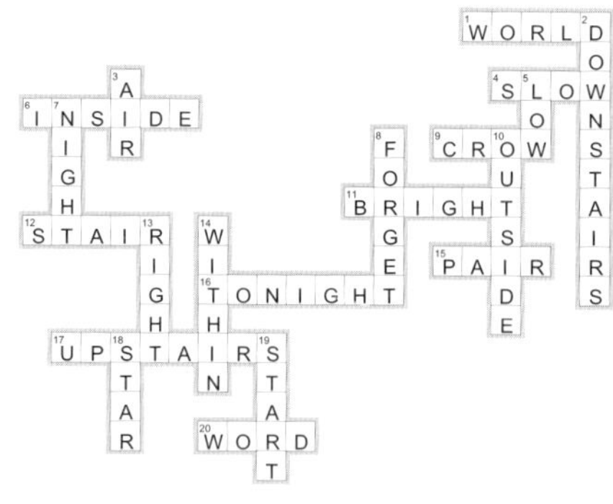

Letter = L

Exercise 52a

1) who
2) nor
3) row
4) bow
5) talked
6) walked
7) maid
8) throw
9) why
10) looking

Exercise 52b

11) talking
12) without
13) walking
14) own
15) looked
16) asked
17) sharp
18) which
19) thinking
20) follow

Crossword No 52

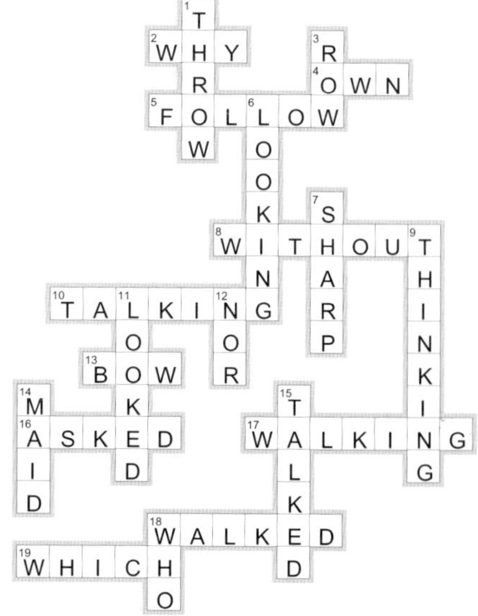

Letter = N

Answers

Exercise 53a

1) filled
2) pork
3) cloud
4) alive
5) north
6) opening
7) along
8) trip
9) doctor
10) speak

Exercise 53b

11) South
12) fork
13) hour
14) loud
15) speaking
16) reading
17) became
18) washed
19) whip
20) opened

Exercise 54a

1) stories
2) teeth
3) tooth
4) babies
5) march
6) green
7) playground
8) football
9) bath
10) having

Exercise 54b

11) ladies
12) giving
13) seen
14) party
15) master
16) living
17) new
18) tiny
19) dance
20) basket

Exercise 55a

1) paw
2) riding
3) jelly
4) carried
5) rice
6) tomorrow
7) merry
8) cherry
9) pence
10) carry

Exercise 55b

11) berries
12) heel
13) shall
14) mice
15) feel
16) jolly
17) once
18) marry
19) cherries
20) berry

Crossword No. 53

Letter = P

Crossword No. 54

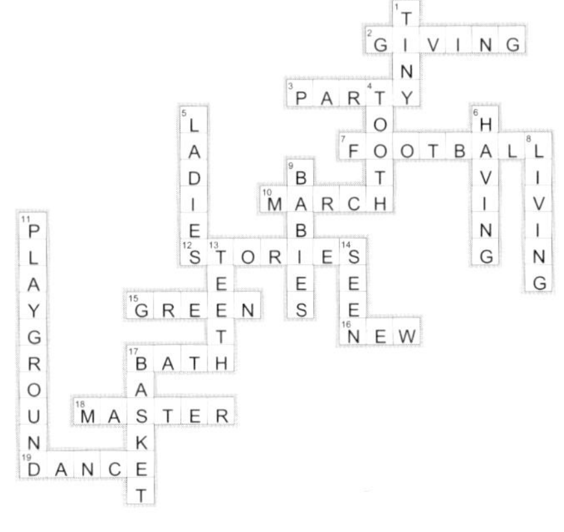

Letter = E

Crossword No. 55

Letter = L

At the Office

1. BRIEFCASE	2. SECRETARY	3. FAN	4. DESK LAMP	5. SKYSCRAPER
6. REPORT	7. POT PLANT	8. FIRST AID KIT	9. LIFT	10. CHART
11. BLIND	12. EXTINGUISHER	13. BIN	14. MANAGER	15. SWIVEL CHAIR

In the Street

1. REMOVAL LORRY	2. CARPORT	3. CHIMNEY	4. BICYCLE	5. SHED
6. HEDGE	7. MOTOR SCOOTER	8. GARAGE	9. LAMP POST	10. 'SOLD' BOARD
11. AERIAL	12. FLOWER BED	13. ROOF	14. BUNGALOW	15. WALL

Answers

Exercise 56a

1) reach
2) raw
3) gay
4) flies
5) please
6) mean
7) easy
8) beads
9) beach
10) crying

Exercise 56b

11) cries
12) warm
13) tried
14) lead
15) great
16) draw
17) bean
18) lean
19) tries
20) cried

Crossword No. 56

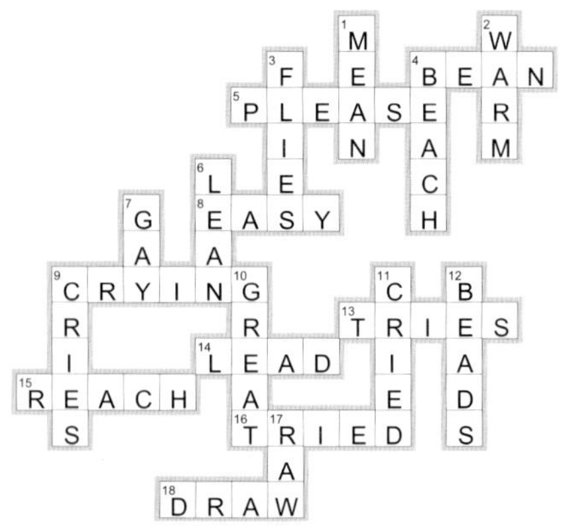

Letter = E

Exercise 57a

1) before
2) dropped
3) two
4) slippers
5) getting
6) anything
7) biggest
8) many
9) better
10) below

Exercise 57b

11) skipping
12) felt
13) dropping
14) fresh
15) running
16) any
17) belong
18) stopped
19) their
20) bigger

Crossword No. 57

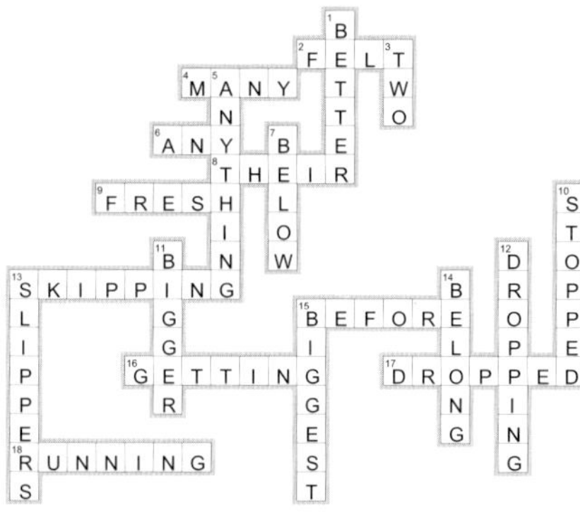

Letter = T

Exercise 58a

1) melt
2) join
3) kept
4) knew
5) bound
6) few
7) oil
8) sound
9) behind
10) off

Exercise 58b

11) pound
12) boil
13) beside
14) point
15) blew
16) know
17) dew
18) drew
19) nothing
20) grew

Crossword No. 58

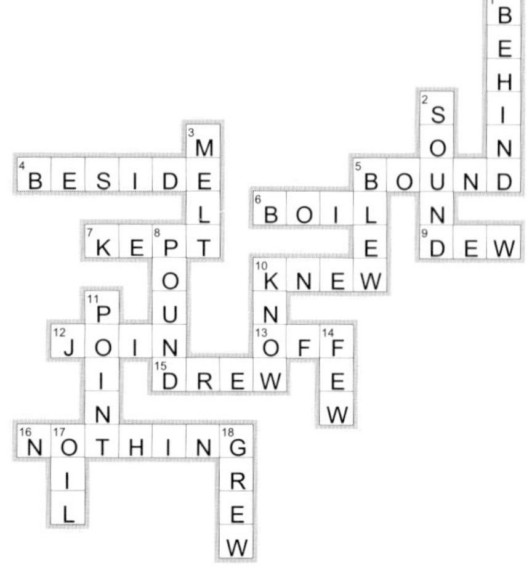

Letter = U

Answers

Exercise 59a

1) thin
2) use
3) those
4) early
5) oxen
6) could
7) would
8) puppy
9) used
10) later

Exercise 59b

11) ox
12) sale
13) desk
14) these
15) key
16) learn
17) cross
18) strong
19) even
20) *Tale*

Crossword No. 59

Letter = E

Exercise 60a

1) *Blue*
2) does
3) played
4) next
5) goes
6) inch
7) drove
8) note
9) Gone
10) stayed

Exercise 60b

11) whole
12) ruler
13) true
14) woke
15) stone
16) bone
17) done
18) clever
19) Uncle
20) number

Crossword No. 60

Letter = C

Exercise 61a

1) strawberries
2) silk
3) ranch
4) porridge
5) corridor
6) forgets
7) wrinkles
8) lettuce
9) arrested
10) some

Exercise 61b

11) actor
12) longer
13) snore
14) finch
15) longest
16) arrived
17) iceberg
18) worm
19) wriggle
20) Emperor

Crossword No. 61

Letter = T

In the Countryside

1. RABBIT	2. FOOTPATH	3. WOOD	4. FOX	5. KESTREL
6. BADGER	7. STILE	8. WINDMILL	9. RETRIEVER	10. STREAM
11. BRIDGE	12. FLASK	13. RAMBLERS	14. DEER	15. MOLE

In the High Street

1. FLORIST	2. DRAIN	3. NEWSAGENT	4. KERB	5. BUTCHER
6. SUPERMARKET	7. CARRIER BAG	8. ROADWORKS	9. GREENGROCER	10. BANK
11. IRONMONGER	12. STREETLIGHT	13. CROSSING	14. PUSHCHAIR	15. LORRY

Answers

Exercise 62a

 1) television
 2) kindly
 3) trapeze
 4) mackintosh
 5) slowly
 6) loudly
 7) tallest
 8) juggler
 9) blackboard
10) kicked

Exercise 62b

11) suddenly
12) pinch
13) happily
14) ballet
15) honestly
16) roller
17) called
18) acrobat
19) jacket
20) tidily

Crossword No. 62

Letter = S

Exercise 63a

 1) fastened
 2) sharpened
 3) caravan
 4) frightened
 5) entered
 6) sadly
 7) travelled
 8) handful
 9) gently
10) poorly

Exercise 63b

11) suitcase
12) roared
13) wellington boots
14) clapping
15) sleeping-bag
16) roof-rack
17) quietly
18) prayed
19) listened
20) dresses

Crossword No. 63

Letter = R

Exercise 64a

 1) bull
 2) ringmaster
 3) suite
 4) celery
 5) orchestra
 6) scales
 7) disappointed
 8) sand-castle
 9) petal
10) yacht

Exercise 64b

11) queue
12) leopard
13) goal
14) hopping
15) drummer
16) rolling-pin
17) apples
18) seagull
19) hole
20) rubbing

Crossword No. 64

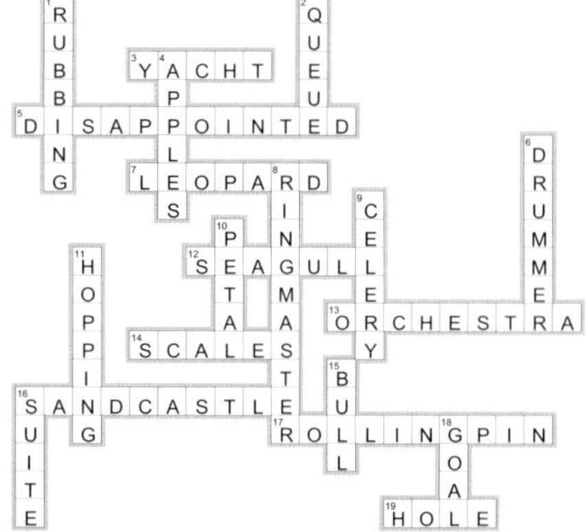

Letter = P

Answers

Exercise 65a
1) matches
2) swimsuit
3) nibble
4) coins
5) stitches
6) wrapped
7) clouds
8) scarecrow
9) beetle
10) bomber

Exercise 65b
11) plumber
12) snuggle
13) stork
14) waddle
15) store
16) waiter
17) aware
18) puddle
19) toys
20) caring

Crossword No. 65

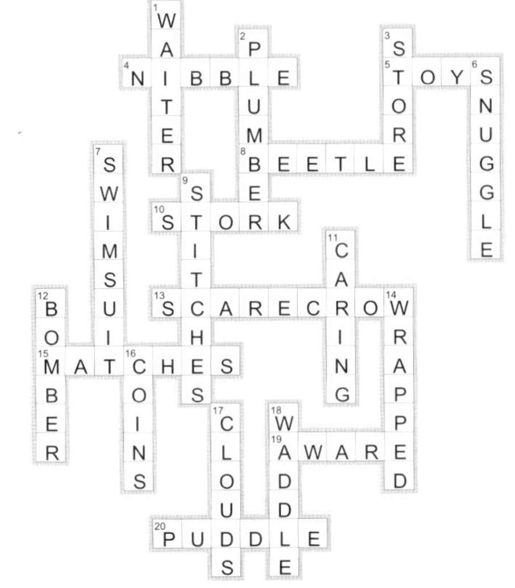

Letter = H

Exercise 66a
1) snarl
2) alley
3) snorkel
4) numb
5) jockey
6) sneak
7) snooker
8) honeycomb
9) knickers
10) mare

Exercise 66b
11) bomb
12) knob
13) snooze
14) sniff
15) snowman
16) snout
17) kidney
18) snack
19) snip
20) sneeze

Crossword No. 66

Letter = E

Exercise 67a
1) moist
2) climber
3) banner
4) adder
5) tomb
6) wealth
7) daddy
8) bellow
9) joiner
10) kennel

Exercise 67b
11) penguin
12) bully
13) haddock
14) cruise
15) manners
16) toilet
17) fluid
18) otter
19) rotten
20) tramp

Crossword No. 67

Letter = A

Answers

Exercise 68a

1) pang
2) lorry
3) hobby
4) prop
5) spray
6) pram
7) barrow
8) prick
9) primrose
10) ravel

Exercise 68b

11) model
12) chemist
13) primary
14) Flinging
15) tinsel
16) level
17) hostel
18) president
19) scrubbing
20) ferry

Crossword No. 68

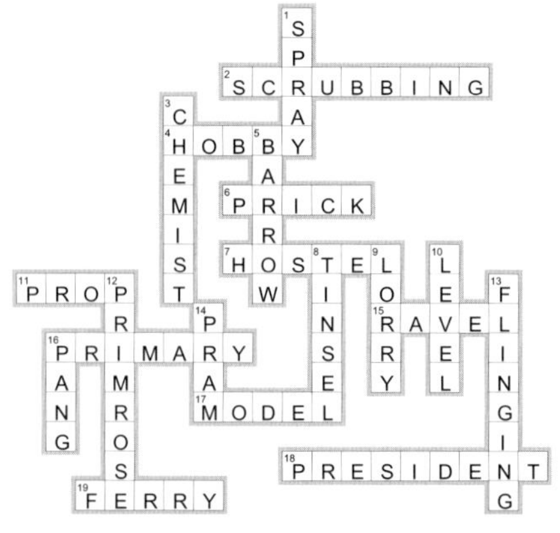

Letter = I

Exercise 69a

1) seventy
2) stew
3) bookcase
4) soya
5) eighteen
6) frightening
7) sighs
8) tangle
9) spoiling
10) seventeen

Exercise 69b

11) coy
12) budge
13) nineteen
14) brew
15) tights
16) sludge
17) bangle
18) wanted
19) ledge
20) achieve

Crossword No. 69

Letter = P

PROGRESS CHARTS

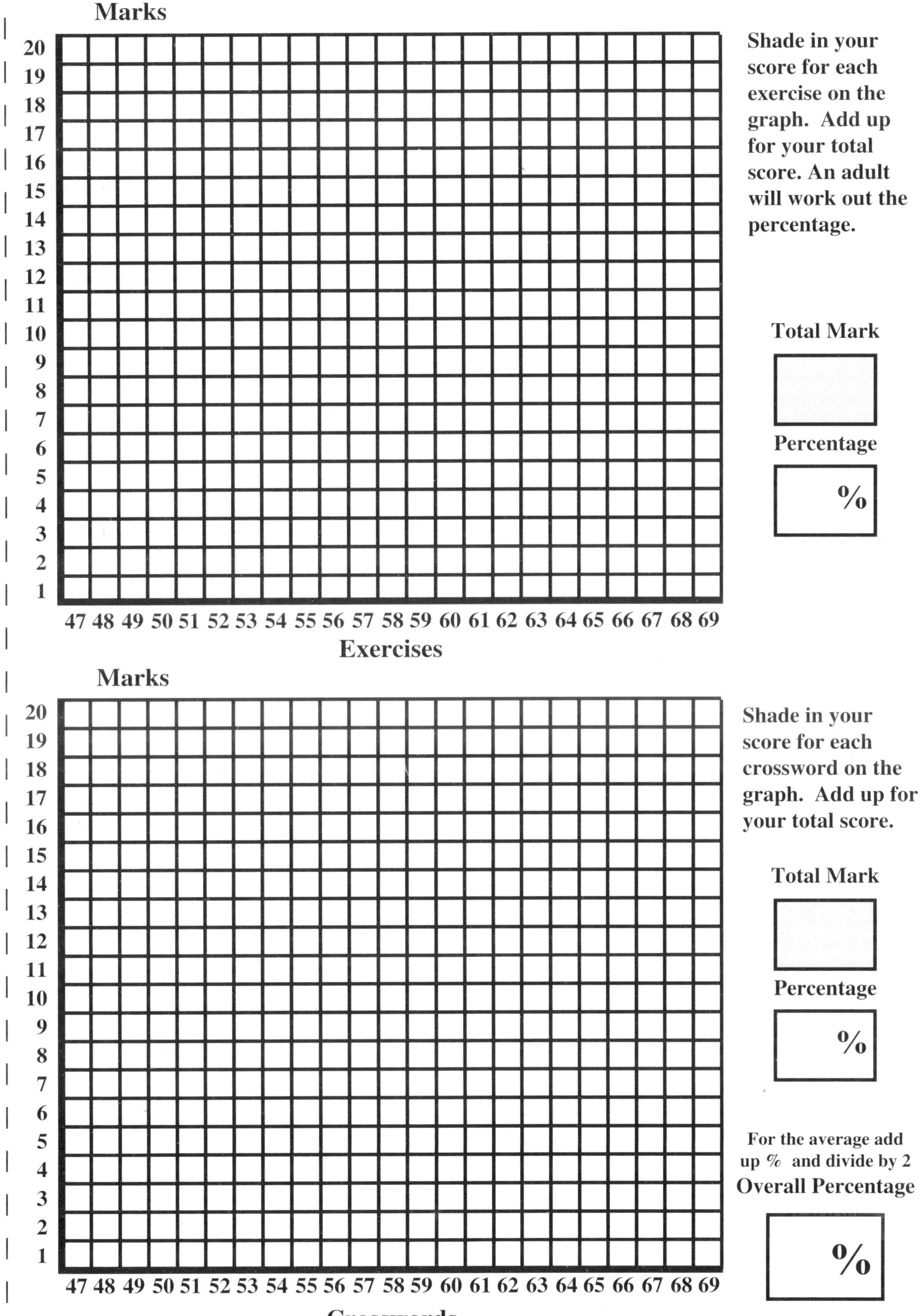

CERTIFICATE
OF
ACHIEVEMENT
(Third)

This certifies ....

has completed **Spelling and Vocabulary Book Three** successfully.

Overall Percentage
Score Achieved

%

Comment.......................................

....

Signed ....

(Teacher/parent/guardian)

Date ....